AF350646

Tattva in understanding life and man

The Hindu Tattva philosophy
with meditative healings and
magical spells instructions

Contents

The Tattvas

Name of Tattva	Meaning in English
Prithvi	Earth
Apas	Water
Agni	Fire
Vayu	Air
Akasha	The Aether

Preface

I can only preface this book with credits to my automatic inspirational writing. I had no idea from chapter to chapter what I could be writing- it was all a mystery to even myself. The words just flew out from my finger into my keyboard of my laptop in creating this book you will read.

Yes, I do have a metaphysical background to rely upon as well which I do find to be very helpful in my writings. I also had done quite a bit of research online on various topics in writing this book. Besides my researched material, the vast part of this book is original and unknown to me before it being written.

I found writing this book to have its moments of growth and many enlightenments. This current book is written in such a way for you to clearly visualize and comprehend many abstract concepts in common English with visual examples. Moreover, to my credit I have experience in writing other metaphysical and esoteric books- I wrote two before this current book you are reading.

Now, do enjoy a good read of my new book regarding the Hindu Tattva. Even though they are Hindu, I tried to bring a Wiccan and European/American application to their understandings of each Tattva.

Enjoy your read!

3

The correction from traditional teachings on this matter

In my own research using my automatic writing skills, I have come to differ with many of the set teachings regarding the four elements, let me explain. Matter is akin to Mulaprakriti, which is the mother of all matter. It is different in the sense that it falls in the realms of delusions- the dream. It is a dream because our source, God, didn't authorize the realities that we all live in. In the tenth Dimension we become Eons or emanations of God's thought.

There was an unauthorized creation make using divine thought as a bases by an Eon- Sophia. Divine thought is one's deepest understanding of our God; and with that thought, amazing things can me made possible- even mis-creations. Our Eon mother- Sophia, in compensation, blesses our realities to make them serve our source and foster the savior principle so we can return back to God;

4

and it is the Christ principle that restores us back to our sanity with God. This principle has countless incarnations; it was the lord Krishna and then Jesus Christ; it had countless incarnations in various innumerable planets; it is not only special to the earth with white Christian people- as was made manifest as Jesus Christ. In fact, it is universal. The lord Vishnu sends out numerous incarnations of saviors in a universal manner to each and every planet where there are souls in darkness.

Back to matter and Mulaprakriti, matter is Mulaprakriti in this unauthorized reality of ours. Mulaprakriti is the mother of matter and is eight imensional and partial of this delusion we are all in. Matter is of the lower Dimensions and more subject to incorrect logic- delusions. Matter does hold its many mysteries as it has been blessed by Sophia and the savior principal for our personal growth and return back to our sanity- God.

Still, our reality, even though blessed, is still unauthorized by God, unfortunately, He doesn't see us here. God sees us as perfect, and with Him in perfections only- not in our present state.

So, matter holds many mysteries according to its blessings, but not what God recognizes. This makes all spiritual progress to be in vain, but we continue anyway in the hope that we can use it to return back to sanity- God. These saviors are here for us all to have faith in and rest upon them to carry us back to God.

Each savior has their own teaching- Jesus teaches forgiveness, to leave the world of it values and of compassion; Krishna the battle of good over bad, and the trusting in your higher mind to carry you over.

So, these mysteries might serve us as they were blessed by the saviors. The highest mystery is of the family unity. The understanding of the family is enough for us to work on, as all other mysteries are less important. Relationships are another mystery. The LDS church- the Mormons- teach of this value.

What the air element is: it's the reflection of the earth element- matter in a mental way. The water element is the misunderstanding of the earth element, and the fire element is our very spirit infused in the lower elements. Without our divine spirit, all life and activities are impossible.

So, if you ever wondered why there is so much evil on our planet and perhaps elsewhere, between the water element symbolizing the delusion and our undeveloped natures, we are just too emotionally reactive and ignorant to have true peace.

Our third d

Dimension is negatively charged- Yin changed anyway which only allows evil to foster.

7

Our savior principles are greatly needed for us to live reasonable lives.

According to Wiccan beliefs, fire, air and water created Earth- matter. This is wrong. Actually, this whole dream of a mis-creation is of the water element. So, it's possible that water is the very first element and holds the mysteries of our reality to be false. In this way, it might serve as an undoing of our mind as we see through our delusions of life. Actually, poverty and a lack of love are delusions. God wishes us all happiness anywhere we are.

Both Jesus and Hindu theosophies teach poverty as a way to God, but are all poor enlightened? No! They have many issues, and should be avoided. Pray for them and make small offerings, but don't take them home. They are learning many important lessons in their poverty.

We all will have our turn being on the streets homeless and seeking mercy and compassion as a lesson of life. It is only a learning path, so never mind those teachings now and win the lotto and seek that perfect lover in this lifetime now! God wishes His Children to be happy.

What is a Tattva, and where did it originate?

The word Tattva, in Sanskrit, means *"that-ness"* or the essence of "That." It denotes a noun and not a verb. Life itself is a verb; what life **has** is its noun- Tattva; these two-go hand and hand together. "That", or "Tattva" usually refers to physical manifestation in co-partnership with life. As life is divine, so is "That"- or to say- Tattva.

We, as life, embody Tattva to project the universes where we live. Tattva have always existed in timelessness but have changed to suit and renew life's demands. Such embodied life becomes the consciousness of the matter or Tattvartha. Tattva consciousness is of elemental life forms that serve higher life forms as their needed realities to manifestations. Tattva is made divine by the blessing of Lord Vishnu' apart from that blessing, Tattva is not divine.

These five root Tattva run in a twenty-second interval with a four-second rest. They animate the "life of all parties" and are present where two or more meet. A Tattva can be invoked and communicated with as they are a semi-divine, subconscious life form. A person usually has at least two pet Tattva that follows them around to serve them.

In comparison, we have Elementals. Elementals are temperamental and moody; they help you when they care to and ignore you as they will. We have come to know them as house spirits. My house spirit can be quite dangerous to others if someone treats me in my home. Tattva are not living aspects of nature with divine qualities; they have no consciousness.

Elementals are mistaken to be Tattva as they behave similarly; however, Elementals have consciousness and are living, while Tattva are inanimate life forms acting as if they are alive. They both are similar in that they flow with the flux; and the flow of nature demands of them both. These Tattva, like elements, can both take on the human form if needed to perform a particular task requested of them directed by higher life forms- Angels, as we call them.

The Tattva, in Indian philosophy, are elements or *principles of reality.* In Samkhya and Shaivite philosophies, Tattva are the basic concepts *to understand the nature of the absolute, the souls, and the Universe.* Samkhya philosophy lists twenty five Tattva, while later Shaivite philosophies extend the number to thirty six. In this book, I have taken up the twenty five Tattva plan. It's better to understand what the Tattva are first. Thus, we need to consider its origins and understand its employments in the Hindu philosophy branch of Samkhya and Shaivite.

This book we are reading now views Samkhya Philosophy in particular. In studying the

Tattva history, we find ourselves in India, where its conception was written in its original form as the Lord Shiva of the Upanishad- the Upanishad being a part of the Rig Vedas- 1600 BCE.

Lord Shiva commands the Tattva in the Upanishads of India. Shiva is lord of the physical and all lower realms beneath what we call spirit. In this way, Tattva is only semi-divine as they are physical and serve the physical. They do not exist in the higher realms of spirit where Vishnu lives. However, lord Krishna must inspire the Tattva and excite them to a semi-divinity to serve the progression of all physical life. The life forms of the humans, animals, fish, elementals, and the physical material realms are all in this flux of divinely directed progressions- a Tattva is just a tool in their performance.

Furthermore, a Tattva in Sanskrit means *principal.* These Tattva or Principal arrays themselves in five aspects: Prithvi/Earth,

13

Apas/Water, Agna/Fire, Vayu/Air, and Akasha/Spirit. These are the five elements that the Demiurges- Lords of creation used to create everything we see and experience. Lord Krishna is the king of these Demiurges.

These Demiurges stand at the edge of time when universes did not exist or might exist; this is the 'true home' of lord Krishna. They will be there when all things return to the void of nothingness again. The B*uddha* is "impure" *Tattva.* There are twenty-five of these impure Tattva. Their energies are mixed with the other four lower elements; they are impure in that they are not solely of Akasha/Spirit. Akasha isn't a Tattva but behaves like a Tattva under the direction of the lord Shiva and Krishna. The fact remains, Akasha would be the only **pure**, so-called, Tattva if not mixed with the lower four.

The downward progressions of Tattva are as follows: The first manifestation from Akasha was view/fire; then came Apas/Water. When Agna and Apas made themselves combust, Prithvi/Earth andVayu/Air were made manifest simultaneously. In this book, we will understand all these Tattva and their intermixing's between them in their manifestness that we have realized, as life. I wrote in commonly placed examples of their nature and service to the living in this book. I hope you might be able to use them in magic, form a better understanding of yourselves, and life, as we know it.

Jainism today still employs these five Tattva/ Principles in their meditationsand magic. In the second to the fifth century A.D, the Jain book *Tattvārthasūtra*, meaning "On the Nature" (Artha) of Reality (Tattva)- On the nature of reality was written; this book contains three hundred and fifty sutras and has over ten chapters. Since the fifth century, the text has attracted numerous commentaries, translations, and interpretations. The

15

book's purpose is to unfold these principles of love to "*helping one another in life*".

Regarding Jainism, the faith with three main pillars are:

1. **Jare ahims**: non-violence
2. **Anakantada**: non absolutism,
3. **Aparigraha**: non-attachment.

In India, Jains are honored as being non-violent and peacemakers; they are homogeneous, but friendly to the Indian people; they do business with all people, but socially, they keep to their people in their Janis culture of their communities. We always know a Jain by their happy and joyous smile in public.

Jain philosophy can be described in various ways, but the most acceptable tradition of describing Jain is in terms of the *Tattva* or *fundamentals*. One must know them to progress

16

towards one's liberation. According to central Jain text, Tattvarthsutra, these are:

1. **Jiva**: Souls and living things
2. **Ajiva**: Non-living things
3. **Asrava**: Influx of karma
4. **Bandha**: The bondage of karma
5. **Samvara**: The stoppage of influx of karma
6. **Nirjara**: Shedding of karmab
7. **Moksha**: Liberation or Salvation

Shaivism

In Shaivism, the *Tattva* are in aid to soul's consciousness and his/her/its material existence. They have 36 Tattva of Shaivism divided into three groups;

- ***Shuddha Tattva***

- The first five Tattva are the *shuddha* or 'pure' *Tattva*. They are also the *Tattva* of universal experience.

- ***Shuddha-ashuddha Tattva***

The following seven *Tattva* (6–12) are the *shuddha-ashuddha* or 'pure-impure' *Tattva*. They are the *Tattva* of limited individual experience.

- ***Ashuddha Tattva***

The last twenty-four *Tattva* (13–36) are the *ashuddha* or 'impure' *Tattva*. The first of these is *Prakriti*, which includes the *Tattva* of mental operation, sensible experience, and materiality.

Vaishnavism

Within Puranic kinds of literature and general Vaiṣnava philosophy, *Tattva* is often used to denote specific categories or types of being or energies such as:

18

- ***Vishnu-Tattva:***

The Supreme God. The causative factor of everything, including other Tattva. Unlike Shiva who is their ruler, Vishnu uplifts Tattva to a semi-divine level in their service to all living life forms and realms.

- ***Krishna-Tattva:***

Any incarnation or expansion of Śrī Narayan/ Krishna. Krishna is the bridge between the Divine- Vishnu, and Material- Shiva to fortify Tattva with life so they can serve all living and realms.

- ***Śakti-Tattva:***

The multifarious energies of Śrī Kṛiṣhṇa include his internal potency, Yoga Maya, and material prakṛiti. Here the illusion of life it made manifest however, with a way to see through it with Vishnu's help.

19

- ***Jiva-Tattva:***

The living souls- Jivas. Tattva help one in each incarnation to direct the flow of the manifestation of life.

- ***Śhiva-Tattva:***

Śrī Śhiva- excluding Rudras is not a Jiva. Rudras is in Hindism, Sanskrit. One who drives away evil; one who is praiseworthy. It is also the name and form of Lord Shiva. Yes, Rudras isn't a Jiva as he stands apart for them all but directs them at the same time as he immerses himself in the actions of the Tattva as Shiva- Tattva.

- ***Mahat-Tattva:***

The total material energy *prakriti*. This is the non-divine aspect of Tattva. Prakriti isn't divine like Tattva are but made semi-divine by means of the lord Vishnu to direct the manifestation of life.

Gaudiya Vaishnavism

Main article: Pancha Tattva - Vaishnavism

In Gaudiya Vaishnava philosophy, there are a total of five primary Tattva described in terms of living beings, which are collectively known as the *Pancha Tattva* and described as follows:

Spiritually, there are no differences between these five Tattva, for everything is absolute on the transcendental platform. However, there are also varieties in the spiritual world. To taste these spiritual varieties, one should distinguish between them.

Mahabhuta or Five Elements and that the *pañcamakara* is a vulgar term for the *pañca Tattva* and affirms that this is cognate with Ganapuja: Worship with the Pañca Tattva generally takes place in a Chakra- circle composed of men and women, Sadhakas and Sadhikas, Bhairavas and Bhairavis sitting in a circle, the Shakti being on the Sadhaka's left. Hence it is called Chakra puja. In this unique setting, we have:

A Lord of the Chakra - *Chakreshvara* - presides, sitting with his Shakti in the center. During the Chakra, there was no distinction of caste, excluding Pashus of any caste. There are various kinds of Chakra -- productive, it is said, of differing fruits for the participator. As amongst Tantrik Sadhakas, we come across the high, the low and mere pretenders. The Chakras vary in characteristics from the Tattva-chakra to the Brahma-Kailas and the Bhairavi-chakra, as described in Mahanirvana (VII. 153). Instead of wine, the householder of milk, sugar, and honey called Madhura Traya, instead of the sexual union, meditation upon the Lotus Feet of the Divine Mother with Mantra.

The ritual of Chakras that will not be approved includes Cudacakra, Anandabhuvana-yoga, and others referred to later. "Chakrapuja" is cognate with Ganachakra or Ganachakrapuja.

The names and forms (Nama-rupa) and the appearances you see outside are all effects of Maya. Maya is Avyakta (hidden, unmanifested); Avyakriti (undifferentiated). It is the indescribable power of Lord Anirvachaniya, being the equilibrium of Sattva (purity), Rajas (passion), and Tamas (inertia). This equilibrium is disturbed by the will of the Lord to give fruits to the Karmas of Jivas. This world projects at the beginning of the Maha Kalpa. Brahman thought:

"These indeed are the worlds; I shall create the protectors for the worlds." He only gathered the Purusha (Hiranyagarbha) out of the water and fashioned him. He heated them with the heat of meditation (Aikshanta). He was heated with heart burst out; from the heat, the mind came from the

23

mind, the moon, the presiding deity of the mind. The heart is the seat of the mind. So, the mind came out when the heart burst out.

In Samadhi, the mind goes to its original seat, the heart. "In sleep, he rests in the heart with a veil of ignorance between the mind and the Brahman (Aitareya Upanishad 1-3-4). "From the Avyaktam or the unmanifested (Maya), the Mahat Tattva comes out first, just as the sprout shoots out from the seed in the ground. From Mahat proceeds Ahankara. Then mind senses, prana, and Tanmatras. Then the external Universe is created out of the five gross elements".

For a better sense of orientation, we will focus on the Philosophy used in this book- **Samkhya-** the study of twenty-five Tattva(s). The other listed form is printed to offer a broader understanding of the Tattva(s) using other philosophies.

Samkhya (Sanskrit:साङ्ख्य),

(IAST: *sāṅkhya*) is a dualistic *āstika* school of Indian philosophy, regarding reality in human experience as being constituted by two ultimate independent principles, *puruṣa* 'consciousness' or' spirit'; and *prakṛiti*, 'cognition, mind, and emotions, **nature** or matter'. Tattva are understood to be an 'aspect of nature' in this scheme, but a larger universal scene of nature that reaches beyond our little planet.

Prakriti and mind, cognition and emotions are all seen as not divine. Our consciousness ends in the thirteenth Dimension and Mind ends in the eighth Dimension; and Emotions in the sixth Dimension. Being that said, they are not divine but lower tools of the lower man of Shiva's realms. I urge you all to think in terms of a Vishnu way of thinking- the Divine!

Puruṣa is witness consciousness- it is absolute, independent, free, unknowable through

25

other agencies, above any experience by mind or senses, and beyond words or explanations. Purusa remains pure as a non-attributing consciousness, where no appeals can qualify Purusha or be substantial or objectified. Purusa, is first realized in the fourteen Dimensions where all self-consciousness is dropped. Hinduism refers to Purusha as the soul of the universe, the universal spirit present everywhere, in everything and everyone, all the time. Purusha is the Universal Principle that is eternal, indestructible, without form, and all-pervasive. Witness consciousness is not self-consciousness but is totally experiential in its nature.

Unmanifest *prakriti* is the primordial matter. It is inactive and unconscious and consists of an equilibrium of the three *guṇas'* qualities, innate tendencies' namely *sattva, rajas*, and *tamas*. When Prakṛiti encounters Purusha, this equilibrium is disturbed. Prakriti becomes manifest, evolving twenty-three Tattva, namely *"intellect -buddhi,"* *"mahat-, ego"*, *"ahamkara mind"*, *"manas-* the five sensory capacities; the five action capacities; and the five "subtle elements", "modes of sensory content" *tanmatras.* The five "gross elements", "forms of perceptual objects" (Earth, water, fire, air, and spirit) emerge, giving rise to the manifestation of sensory experience and cognition). Here we see the demiurges of the fourteenth Dimension making manifest the lower thirteen Dimensions with Dimension two to seven being material.

Jiva, 'a living being' is a state where *Purusha* bondes to *Prakriti.* The human experience is an interplay of *Purusha-Prakriti*; Purusha being conscious of the various combinations of cognitive activities. The end of the bondage of Purusha to Prakriti is called liberation or kaivalya- *Isolation-* by the Samkhya school. Loneliness, depression, and isolation are both gifts not to be overlooked. They guide one to their truest

27

self in time. We must drop out lived values for higher ones or the old in a higher form.

This *Isolation* may come as an intruder to some, but in one's middle to late ages and older, it serves as the healing of the whole life. I find it very sad that some seniors are bored with seeking companionship from family and friends to shield them from their loneliness. I was lonely in my twenties, but in my thirties to early fifties, I found myself with many interests and endeavors. Now in my early sixties, I love being alone. I study German and French; I am improving my Italian vocabulary and expressions. I practice the piano, violin, and harp by writing books studying Quantum Theory; composing a Harp sheet music book and I love astrology as well. I've become aware that much math is needed for Quantum like Trigonometry, Physics, Linear Algebra, and essential Calculus I, II, III. Now, I need more time in the day for all my interests. To my mind, I'm a renaissance man and an enlightened Virgo. Yes, I can have a partner, but that partner must be of a higher level of experience, not witnessed before in my life.

Yes, I socialize in bars and Jazz Clubs here in New Orleans, but not too much. I prefer to remain home with my dog, cat, and teddy bear at night, staying online or practicing my instruments. I find YouTube to be very educational. New Orleans has Art Museums, but for a larger body of real Art, I had to travel for five and a half hours with my dog to Houston, Tx to the Houston Art Museum.

I enjoyed the European and American Art collections gathered donated by local wealthy families in town there. I wish I had more friends to talk to over the phone and to haverelationships with, though. One question I ask myself is: Could a close relationship impose on my privacy? I wrote about my interest in showing you all that very close companionships and sexual involvement in later life could hold us back from gaining self-knowledge incoming to know the Self better. If a partner might be right for me, that partner must be on the same path or growth and respect my privacy.

Yes, my Isolation serves me- if I want to see people, I'll go to a Jazz Club, a potluck dinner, or a local bar. Walking around alone on Bourbon Street in the French Quarter is fun too. I meet up with so many friendly shop attendants in town to chat with. I say: If you know yourself, you are never lonely.

I recall being very lonely in my youth and finding comfort with bad associations. Getting over codependency and accepting the Self was my significant life accomplishment. One good thing about my childhood and early adult life was that I traveled to many foreign cities, exotic countries, and resorts.

Yes, I was attractive, so sex was easy. However, I was far too confused and mistrustful to maintain an intimate relationship with a partner in

30

my youth. As I got older, I did have love relationships. My military experience seemed disastrous; however, I gained disability pay with a reasonable monthly check for my service due to service connection disabilities acquired. By the age of sixty-two, I could not have believed so much of my life was over, but I am shocked to find out how much I have going for myself currently. Life expectancy is rising each year, so I have a lot of living more to do!

My father died of bladder cancer. I always had a similar bladder as him. He had senile dementia. I recently learned that 15 minutes in sunshine fights dementia. So, yes, the *Isolation* of the Samkhya school is a good thing. I do hope that all young people can find yourselves toward their middle to late ages as I do now.

Returning to the Hindu creation story in the Rig Vedas, we see that creation conceived in the bowl of Cosmic Aetheria. The second Dimension's

31

creative energies made a unique sound wave focusing to a central focal point, or the dot Bindu in Sanskrit rested in the first Dimension. This Bindu-dot contained the combined powers of both the male Shiva and the female Shakti, like a dicotyledonous seed that produced the two separate entities, Shiva, and Shakti. The union of these two resulted in the rest of the creative unfolding. Thus, one can observe that whatever exists in this creation can be traced back to this primeval Naad. 'Naad' means sound, and 'yoga' means union.

The basic principle behind this is the union with the inner Brahma God through Shabda Brahma (divine sound) and awakening its might. The concept has been in existence since Vedic times but has been forgotten ever since. The five Tattva(s) and the three Gunas were created from that timeless moment. The chanting of OM and using the Tibetan sing bowl may return you to the Naad, where the order brought to chaos can be found. I use piano composing as my Naad. I feel so much better and more relaxed after working on my music.

The **Gunas are Sattva, Rajas, and Tomas.** The word in Sanskrit means qualities. Sattva is the sweet, passive female, Rajas is active and male, and Tomas is inert evil or material. Tomas is seen as unfavorable or resisting the nature of akasha- spirit. There is also the last- A sattva which is a type of good that only advanced souls may understand and explains in detail the world's evil and why it must be.

In Hinduism, the religion chiefly of India, OM is a sacred syllable considered to be the greatest of all the mantras or sacred formulas. The syllable O*m* is composed of the three sounds *a-u-m* in Sanskrit with the vowels *a* and *u* coalesce to become *o*, which represent several important triads: the three worlds of Earth, atmosphere, and heaven; thought, speech, and action; the three qualities *Gunas* of the matter: goodness, passion, and darkness; and the three sacred Vedic scriptures "Rigveda, Yajurveda, and Samaveda". Thus, *Om* mystically embodies the essence of the entire Universe. It is uttered at the beginning and end of Hindu prayers, chants, and meditation. It is also freely used in Buddhist terms to mark the beginning of a text in a manuscript or an inscription.

The syllable is discussed in several of the Upanishad's speculative philosophical texts, forming the entire subject matter of one, the Mandukya Upanishad- all is Atma or Brahamn. In verses 3 to 6, the Mandukya Upanishad enumerates four states of consciousness: wakefulness, dream, deep sleep, and the state of ekatma (being one with Self, the oneness of Self). These four are A + U + M + "without an element" respectively; it is used in the practice of Yoga and is related to techniques of auditory meditation.

In the Puranas, the syllable is put to sectarian use. The Shaivites mark the *lingam*, or sign of

34

Shiva, with the symbol for O*m*. In contrast, the Vaishnavites identify the three sounds as referring to a trinity composed of Vishnu, his wife Shri (Lakshmi), and the worshipper.

The Naad is most defiantly the OM. You may chant the OM with a *Tibetan Singing Bowl* in those suites you. Between the two, I hope you melt into the birth of the Universe of time and space.

To add a Hindu element to this essay:

Adi Shankara wrote a treatise on this theory, titled *"Pancikaranam"*, which was elaborated by his disciple Sureshvaracharya, and later commented upon in 2400 slokas byRamananda Saraswati, a disciple of Ramabhadra, and in 160 slokas by AnandaGiri, a disciple of Suddhananda Yati. The Chandogya Upanishad teaches the doctrine of tripartition (*trivṛtkaraṇa*) from which developed the Vedantic theory of *pancikarana* concerning the creation of the transformed evolutes of the original elements; this theory is found narrated to Narada in the *Srimad Devi Bhagavatam.*

Pancikarana is the creation of the elements *bhūtasarga* by a process in which subtle matter or the prior stage of matter transforms itself into the gross matter. Intelligence is the subtle manifestation of consciousness and matter is its gross manifestation.

Pancikarana is the "quintuple" of the primary/primordial five subtle elements. The subtle elements remain *tanmātrā*. During *pancikarana,* each is firstly divided into two halves, one part of which was further divided into four parts, equal to 1/8th parts of each subtle element, which then recombined with the undivided halves of each element. Thus, each of the five gross elements *pañcabhūta* consists of half of the corresponding subtle element and four fractions from the other four subtle elements. Accordingly, each gross element has a fivefold composition. It

36

was also assumed that this process of division and recombination continually until grosser elements are produced in a continuous unending process. The processes of *Srishti,* 'creation', *Stithi,* 'sustenance', and *Samhara* 'dissolution'- which is continual and without change or interruption.

Pancikarana- Pancikarana is the creation of the elements (bhūtasarga) by a process in which subtle matter (or the prior stage of matter) transforms itself into gross matter. Pancikarana involves one-half of the original subtle element mixed up with 1/8th part of each other. Original subtle elements that produces the gross elements of the subtle element contributing itself to one half. When gross elements are produced, consciousness enters these elements as their presiding deities, then comes the feeling of egoism (I-ness) identifying with the body. Gross elements solidify and assume forms as per their fundamental qualities.

The Gunas

1. **Rajas:** activity, movement, restlessness, passion
2. **Tamas:** rigidity, laziness, darkness, ignorance
3. **Sattva:** harmony, light, purity, knowledge

Tattva and Gunas are the primordial forces that influence physical and astral planes. They influence all forms of life physically, psychically, and spiritually from the beginning of their earthly existence to their end. Through the multi-layered combinations of these elemental powers, the human body, with its highly complex organ, nerve, and brain functions, comes into existence, and the psyche and mind are formed

The diverse interactions between the five gross Tattva, which form the physical body, are known as Prakriti (natural forces). There are twenty five Prakritis that influence and regulate the systems of the body.

The Tattva flowing aimlessly around in space are independent forces without visible effect. Only when several of these primordial, undirected forces are concentrated to one point will something qualitative new be produced. However, an assembly point must first be formed so the energy can be focused and assimilated. The most highly developed and most powerful center on Earth is the human. So, just as bees collect around the queen bee, all forces and Tattva follow when the Ātma enters the embryo. For a human form to be constructed, the orderly combination of many effects is necessary. In the same way, but at a lower intensity, animal and plant life come into being.

The Cosmic forces are collected within the human body at the Chakras' central points. These function like powerful power stations. They draw in cosmic energy, transform, store, and

39

distribute it, and then radiate it again into the Cosmos.

The Tattva that combined form the human body dwell with the soul and are detached from one another at death and return to the Cosmos. The soul wanders, waiting to produce a new form again under suitable conditions. This cycle is called "*Chorasi Ka Chakra*", "The Wheel of Rebirth and Death."

According to Indian philosophy, there are 8.4 million living beings divided into three categories: Nabha Chara, Thala Chara, And Jala Chara- living beings that exist in the air, those that live on or under the Earth, and those that live in the water. They are further divided into four different classifications according to their method of birth into these three earthly spheres:

1. **Jarāyuja**: in the womb (humans and mammals)

2. **Andaja**: in a hatched egg (birds, reptiles, fish, etc).

3. **Svedaja**: through division (lower forms of life, bacteria, etc.)

4. **Udbhijja**: through seed (vegetation)

Each of these groups has certain aptitudes and abilities called Kalā in Sanskrit. Plants possess one Kalā; lower life forms two, egg-laying animals three, and mammals and humans four. While plants and animals remain at the level of their genesis, humans can develop up to sixteen Kalā through exercises, concentration, and following the principles of Yoga. They can acquire twelve supernatural powers in addition to their four natural aptitudes.

Therefore, evolving to the human level is the most remarkable advantage for the soul. Enabling this, with God's grace, innumerable Cosmic powers act in combination, and this joining is comparable to a great fire. Qualitatively the souls of all beings

41

are the same: they are differentiated only in the degree of their development. A small candle flame is "fire", but a brighter light, a more concentrated power, results from combining several flames. Human life is more intensive and conscious than animals and distinguished from all other life forms through the gift of the intellect (Buddhi).

Without faltering, the wheel of rebirth keeps turning, and the soul wanders through the circle of existence driven by God's plan and Karmas (actions). Human life offers the only possibility of ending this cycle. The cyclic laws of nature also bind humans. However, with the help of the intellect, they can explore the world, themselves, and the supernatural powers. That is why they can emerge from the cycle of rebirth and, consequently, help others. Our current concept of an only godhead has been invented between the two influences. In the Hindu faith, the eldest and highest Godhead is a mere abstract description, not a God to be worshipped. The West has developed but on a different level than the Juana school in India.

Only humans are capable of understanding "What God is". Only humans can realize God. Monotheism originated with the Eighteenth Dynasty's tenth ruler Pharaoh Akhenaten between the years 1353 to 1336. Akhenaten wrote most of the Hebrew Psalms under the of Aten. Akhenaten helped the Jewish faith in ways that the Jews won't admit. Zoroastrianism had the second most considerable influence on Judaism with its battles between good and evil. Their influence caused the Jews to be more moralistic. Also, many of the Jewish cleanliness laws have Egyptian origins.

The practice of Yoga supports and accelerates the development of humans as it imparts to their knowledge of the proper Dimension of earthly life, its purpose, and potential. The evolution of consciousness attains fulfillment in the divine state of Samādhi, where Knower, Knowledge, and

43

the Object of Knowledge become one. Since the beginning of its existence, the individual Self has sought to gain knowledge about- the Self. While in Samādhi, the Self is recognized and seen as the Knower. The objectives of knowledge are the same. So begins the blissful experience of unity, displacing the wrongly cherished illusion of duality.

This supreme knowledge is transmitted through two spiritual Tattva, Anupada Tattva And Ādi Tattva. Anupama Tattva (Guru Tattva) is the universal, divine principle that leads the creation from "darkness into light"- from unconscious to conscious existence. Ādi Tattva is the divine Self, Ātmā. Therefore, it is also called Ātma Tattva or Ātma Gyāna. Self-Realized Yoga masters are known as *Brahmanishta Shrotria*, the knowers of Brahman, and *Tattva Darshi*, the knowers of the Tattva. Their knowledge and experiences are unlimited; they transcend time, space, and intellect.

44

One who possesses self-knowledge and knowledge of the Tattva has acquired the highest knowledge realizable by a human. With this, one becomes the "knower of God" (Brahma Gyāni), and the Self merges into the divine consciousness and becomes one with God. The Earth elements come fifth because it evolves out of each of the other four elements, Aether, Air, Fire, and Water, containing the essence of these elements within it.

The Five Elements- Explained

With Albert Einstein's formula, $e = mc^2$, Where E is Fire- energy, M is mass- matter, and C is Air or light speed. Let us consider the Water/Fire mysterious elements in how they form a bridge between Air and Earth, with Fire being its catalyst. Water is the key to life on Earth, with its heart in the Fire element. Water and Fire are paired together in creation to produce all things. Aether is the mother of all four elements, akin to the Fire element. The water element is beyond logical explanations to write about. The human psyche is of this water element and holds the key to understanding. So, the water element is the logistical hand of creation, withholding the purpose and desire for its conceptions. The water element was unmanifested and even came before Aether but is reflected in Aether as the flow down approaches manifestations. The water element is the home of all souls to be incarnated. The Fire element is the home of all spirits that came before souls.

In lower creations, the water element came first, but its higher creations were the fire element akin to Aether. Vishnu is Fire, and Shiva is water in the Upanishads. Aether reflects both elements as their siblings on the monadic level. The Earth element is the child of all four- Fire, Water, Earth, and Air houses the Aethers Tattva. Aether is our blessing like no other element can. Aether is positively charged, but Earth is negatively charged. Both Earth and Water are negative, and Fire and Air are positive. Aether works best, and it is reflected in the higher elements of Fire and Air, but it's housed there at its heart. The Fire element is the doorway to Aether, though to bring in new life and energies to the Earth element as a bridge. The Water element guarantees the success of the formations to our original design and purpose for all life everywhere in the lower quadrant of Shiva.

What is Aether? Aether is the first law of physics- gravity. But is Aether really gravity, or does it respond as gravity? We are revolving around our Godhead, then our sources- God; this makes Aether a divine element but not really an element at all but a law.

Aether is a product of the *One Monad we all share in life*. We are all grouped under the one Monad of life. We call it God, but we have mistaken it by thinking that it is the one the only God when, in fact, it isn't at all. This group Monad is of a seventh Dimension, but is also rooted in the ninth Dimension. This Monad oversees all lower life. We have a unique ninth-Dimension Monad; however, it is merely an aspect of the One in the Ninth Dimension. We are all Gods in the seventh Dimension, but under one rooted force that joins all life below in the ninth Dimension.

Such a ninth dimensional Monad is a mere lower reflection of the One, and only One Monad of all life everywhere. In esoteric Christianity, we call the rotation around the One collectively as- The Christ.

The seventh Dimension is where our God's name is. We use this God's name to grow in a particular manner. This God name is how we view God in a name form alone. The ninth dimensional lords have a loose governing force over us but root us in what we can call- The Divine. Between the two, the God force that we possess functions quite well.

The ninth Dimension is where we meet Aether for the first time. The Aether element's source is in this one-ninth dimensional Monad. Aether, on the highest level, is life itself, and it is out of reach. Yes, the Aether touches our soul but in an impure manner. It will only be pure then we can incarnation to the ninth Dimensions worlds of bliss and wonder.

49

We gain *sweet atoms* here on Earth through Aether embedded in the Earth element. Aether is stabilized and made productive in the Earth element. That is why great and high angels for high Dimensions need to revitalize themselves here in the physical from time to time to regain a sense of structure and a newly found vitality. Even eightth dimensional spirits need to incarnate to renew. Only above the eight are we free of incarnations downward from high places. What we may deem physical, are the Dimensions of multiverses from the second Dimension to the seventh, which is full of inhabitable realms of life.

Returning to the Hindu creation story in the Rig Vedas, we see that creation is conceived in the bowl of the cosmic Aether. The second Dimension's creative energies of unique sound waves were focused on a central focal point, or to say the Bindu-dot in Sanskrit rested in the first Dimension. This Bindu-dot contained the combined powers of the male Shiva and the female Shakti, like a dicotyledonous seed that produced the two separate entities, Shiva and Shakti. The union of these two resulted in the rest of the creative unfolding.

Thus, one can observe that whatever exists in this creation can be traced back to this primeval Naad. 'Naad' means sound, and 'yoga' means union. The basic principle behind this is the union with the inner Brahma God through Shabda Brahma (divine sound) and awakening its might. The concept has existed since Vedic times but has been forgotten ever since. The five Tattva(s) and the three Gunas were created from that timeless moment. The chanting of OM and using the Tibetan sing bowl may return you to the Naad, where order in chaos can be found. I use piano composing as my Naad. I feel so much better and more relaxed after working on my music.

The Gunas are Satva, Rajas, and Tomas. The word in Sanskrit means *qualities*. Sattva is the

51

sweet or sound female, Rajas is active and male, and Tomas is evil or material. Tomas is seen as unfavorable or resisting the nature of akasha- spirit. There is also the last- A sattva, which is a good that only advanced souls possess can understand and explain the world of evil and why it must be so.

In Hinduism and other religions, chiefly in India, the OM is a sacred syllable considered the greatest of all the mantras or sacred formulas. The syllable *om* is composed of the three sounds *a-u-m* in Sanskrit; the vowels *a* and *u* coalesce to become *o*, which represent several important triads: the three worlds of Earth, atmosphere, and heaven; thought, speech, and action; the three qualities *Gunas* of the matter: goodness, passion, and darkness; and the three sacred Vedic scriptures "Rigveda, Yajurveda, and Samaveda." Thus, *om* mystically embodies the essence of the entire Universe. It is uttered at the beginning and end of Hindu prayers, chants, and meditation. It is

52

also freely used in Buddhist terms to mark the beginning of a text in a manuscript or an inscription.

The syllable is discussed in many of the speculative philosophical texts of the Upanishad, forming the whole topic of the Mandukya Upanishad. It is used in the practice of Yoga and is related to techniques of auditory meditation. In the Puranas, the syllable is put to sectarian use. The Shaivites mark the *lingam*, or sign of Shiva, with the symbol for *om*. In contrast, the Vaishnavites identify the three sounds as referring to a trinity composed of Vishnu, his wife Shri (Lakshmi), and the worshipper.

The Naad is most defiantly the OM. You may chant the OM with a *Tibetan Singing Bowl* in those suites you. In between, I hope you will merge in the birth of the Universe of time and space.

53

Who is Narmer? Is he the Legendary hero in ancient Egyptian history – Menon?

Narmer was the 32nd century BC founder of Pharaonic Egypt, and was celebrated throughout the region's ancient period for uniting Upper and Lower Egypt. As the king of Upper Egypt, Narmer led a campaign sometime around 3200 BC to conquer the northern kingdom of Lower Egypt, though this date is uncertain.

Narmer is a crucial character in Egyptian history. He was the founder of Dynasty I and, therefore, the first pharaoh of Ancient Egypt; this occurred around 3050 BC, and his reign lasted for six decades, according to sources such as Herodotus and Sincero. Menes was assigned to him as a throne name when he ascended to the throne of Upper Egypt.

I had many incarnations during the period; I later incarnated in a late dynastic time to serve at the temple of Subek/Heru in today's Kom Ombo Egypt. I also recall being a priestess of the goddess Het-Heru/Hathor in many incarnations. When I magically saw the ruins at Kom Ombo, I visited the temple as it was in ancient times and felt heavenly energy coming from it.

Another Menon is an accountant in the ancient Indian court system, but I'm not associated with that system. Yet, the name is related to soldiers of the Greek Trojan wars. I was always very good with my money, even when I had very little. Who knows– I could be wrong.

In my youth, a Spiritualist Church Priest– Reverend Donald Fredricks, told me that Menes/Menon was my spiritual master. A master oversees all my spiritual growth in many realms of existence. Menes is another name for Narmer. I recall having many early dynasty Egyptian past lives and still practicing the old faith myself.

I had very early incarnations in various realms with Menes. I feel that he is the governing force over all my incarnation processes and back again. I hope he can understand that I'm requesting a long pause in carnations and to be left in an Aetheric realm to do good for all living souls.

I didn't want to have the incarnation this time, but my parents needed to have me as their child, so I could grow apart from them in this incarnation. That is good karma to be with– now I wish to win the lotto as a karmic reward, lol.

The Great Mathematicians

1. Pythagoras

Pythagoras lived between 570 and 495 BC. Almost every school child is familiar with his name. His works later influenced other great minds, such as Euclid and Plato. Many consider him one of the first great mathematicians.

He founded the Pythagorean cult to study and advance mathematics actively. Pythagoras' theorem is used in modern measurements, though some doubt whether Pythagoras invented the theorem. Many claims that Boudhayan, an Indian mathematician, lived around 800 BC. Boudhayan influenced Pythagoras' complete teaching.

However, Pythagoras invented the "Greek Modes" of music theory. These modes were used exclusively until the 1800th century. Many scholars claim that Pythagoras obtained most of the knowledge he is accredited to, from Egypt and

Samaria. The invention of Pi was an Egyptian invention, as the great pyramids could never have been built without its use. Pythagoras is accredited with the invention of Trigonometry. However, trigonometry is needed to work with Pi, so who knows if he is the founder is Trigonometry?

2.   Boudhayan theorem

Boudhayian said: The areas produced separately by the length and the breadth of a rectangle together equal the areas created by the diagonal. The diagonal and sides referred to, are those of a rectangle, and the areas are those of the squares having these line segments as their sides. Hence, we have proved the Pythagorean Theorem.

One of the rules in Boudhayan Sulba sutras states that a rope stretched along the diagonal length produces an area that the vertical and horizontal sides make together. He may have invented Pi

58

before the Egyptians, but it was used almost 2000 years before him in Egypt.

3.   Archimedes

Archimedes was born in 287 BC and is considered one of the greatest mathematicians ever. He laid the foundation of several crucial mathematical concepts at the root of modern mathematics. Archimedes anticipated modern calculus by applying the concepts of infinitesimals. He used exhaustive methods to prove many geometrical theorems, such as the area of a circle, the surface area, and the area under a parabola. He also derived an accurate approximation of Pi using the method of exhaustion.

4.   Euclid

Euclid's mathematical treatise *Elements* is still one of the most influential works in the history of mathematics. The ancient Greek mathematician founded geometry; his other works include the

Euclidean algorithm, perfect numbers, and the fundamental theorem of arithmetic. He has had the most significant influence on the advancement of mathematics.

5.   Imhotep

Imhotep was one of the chancellors of the Pharaoh Djoser, and the high priest of the sun god Ra. He was the architect who designed the Pyramid of Djoser.

No one can be sure about Imhotep's early life because no text from his lifetime mentions anything about his achievements. Ten centuries after his death, the world has begun to know his abilities in Architecture and engineering.

He was also a magician, poet, and judge. The first pyramid of Djoser was built during the third dynasty, around 2630 BC–2611 BC, at Saqqara, northwest of Memphis. Being that it would have been impossible to design and build Djoser Pyramid without the knowledge of Pi, Imhotep was the first master mathematician the world had ever experienced.

Imhotep was also a physician, and his last legion was revived by the philosopher **Hermes Trismegistus.** To my research, Imhotep influenced the worship of Tahuti– Thoth in Greek. Imhotep's writing did not last long. The Greeks studied Imhotep quite a bit, and wrote many books in his name years after his death. For all we know, perhaps he invented Pi and an early form of trigonometry.

How to use a Tattva in magic or meditation?

The technique I learned from the Hermetic Order of the Golden Dawn is the best way to use Tattva's images. In their meditation, one stares at one chosen Tattva image for one minute and then looks away. Your eyes will automatically manifest their relative opposite reflection floating in hyperspace before your face.

That opposite reflection serves as a doorway for us to enter our chosen Tattva experience; from there, elementals will guide us to a unique experience with the Tattva energy invoked. Such energy will mesh with our psyche to produce the unique clairvoyant expertise of color and lights, with a psychic message to counsel us in the healing needed for that chosen Tattva.

Another way is to use a candle of the same color value as the Tattva decorated with metallic paint. For example– for the water of Prithvi: use a blue candle and carve a square box on the candle's stomach. Then with metallic paint, design a crescent moon as it lies down with silver metallic paint. Try to design it exactly like the image on paper or in a book. Chant its Hindi name while ringing a singing OM bowl, from Sanskrit- Apas- three times, then light the candle and chant the divine name three more times. Place the water image by the candle as well. The blue candle should be a seven-day novena candle.

Place a cup of water by the candle. Do the above clairvoyant meditation to add essence to your experience with the water. Think about emotions, growth, and relationships. Chanting the Tattva's names often with both techniques/spells' rituals is essential. Go to your prayer at least twice a day to repeat the ritual until the candle burns down. Even the purest priest in India– the Jains practiced magic.

63

Why not you? Wicca has been part of prayer practice and Christian science for over half my life.

Prithvi – Earth

Prithvi Tattva Earth– The Purple and Yellow Square

The choice used by the forefather who derived this earthly Tattva system as designed in purple and yellow has astrological implications: Purple – **Jupiter** (the higher mind); and Yellow – **Mercury** (the lower mind). The two are involved in focusing the mind and expanding simultaneously.

However, considering these contrary forces, realistic thinking is required here on Earth. If the Water element is not in balance, an unrealistic way of thinking and fear will occur; however, if in harmony, the Earth element will be fertile and foster growth. If the fire element is not balanced, reactionary behavior, defensiveness, and territorial thinking could be predomination. If the fire Tattva could be in balance on the Earth, the souls of God would experience righteous rulership; else, unrighteousness with prevail. If the air element did not work in harmony on the planet, poor communication of thought, and a lack of education would incur; however, if the air element should be in balance, the world could be highly educated to resolve all lower imbalances, as mentioned above.

Finally, if the aethereal energy were not in balance, no advanced life can exist on the Earth, and the practice of killing weakening life forms to survive will prevail. Furthermore, no real quality of life will be seen on our planet. That is why the local galactic arm of alien space brothers and sisters cannot get too involved with us. We are just far too primitive and uninvolved, we don't even have a global unifying world government, and we eat meat, currently. Now, if the ethical elements could be in balance here, all our common sense and reasoning would all be of the divine. There would be no more mental illness or life-threatening physical illnesses.

To mention the color scene of Prithvi a bit, the purple hue rules religious interests and royalty. Many older faiths worshipped their Kings and

67

Pharaohs as God's representatives in the flesh. The institution of the Popes is one of the world's oldest traditions going back thousands of years to that first pharaoh. All these lords are relied upon to be the central channel as a connection for the divine to enter local governments.

Yes, I have witnessed Popes and Cardinals react quite humanly and not divine. Cardinal O'Connor of New York City responded just like a victim when he experienced an assassination attempt. If he was divine, he could have empathized with the attacker and not felt like a victim. Pope John Paul was seeking self-glory by making many souls into saints. He hoped he might be elected a saint in time, but he wasn't. The next Pope denounced most of John Paul's so-called saints as regular Catholics.

The current Pope is quite unique, according to most people's opinions. Yes, there were outstanding Popes, Kings, and Pharaohs. I even had incarnations in the Russian royal court system, but I have difficulty recalling them.

What does yellow symbolize in Hinduism? Yellow, in Hinduism, is the color of Lord Vishnu, the color of purity, victory, virtue- and surprisingly- sensuality too, since in spring, in India, unmarried girls wear yellow clothes. Some Hindu tribes believe that yellow can keep evil spirits away. However, we must also consider the Western concept of yellow being the mind.

Moreover, Vishnu, our savior God, is the central godhead in the Prithvi Tattva, who will bring order to chaos if I pray to him. Being ever so stable – Prithvi – it is also unstable. The Earth element has a cold, lifeless nature to it. The great lord Vishnu must send down to the Earth's savior from time to time, like the Buddha, Christ, Mohammed, Hercules, Adonis, the Aten, Lao-tzu, Confucius, and Zoroaster, to inspire us all. I mentioned that Shiva is the lord of the lower realms, but Vishnu is

69

the caretaker of Prithvi as an element to bless it so it can be used to liberate us from its hold. Apart from that element, Shiva is the lord of all the lower realms of humanity.

We are referring to the *physicality* of the Earth Plane in these respects and just how physical it truly is, or, to say – to the touch. According to my research, our planet has experienced two global freezes and more than a few extinctions from meteorite strikes. Who is to say our world has experienced only one ice age when, in fact, it was several? The truth is, our planet is quite unstable, which does influence our psychics.

In a previous book, I wrote - ***Personal Growth in the Multi-dimensional Multiverse,*** that our Earth's Mother doesn't care much about fostering advanced human life. Gaia prefers just plants, animals, and fish life forms only. Gaia does have some patience for us, being that we evolved here. Our parent race – the Elohim

70

impregnated our early human race with their DNA to make us their offsprings, so we worshiped them. These Elohim were seen as ungodly by Gaia, and she chased them away in time. Since most of our DNA was earthly, Gaia took us in as one of her animal life forms initially.

Over 50,000 years ago, we started to work the land for food, and in 12,000 the first civilizations appeared in the Lavine. We are in the atomic age and working toward a world government. Our cities will be levitated platforms that can travel. We also will be in the space station in our Earth's orbit and far away from our home planet. Our earth mother, Gaia, will help us then leave her to her interest – us not being one of them. The Elohim are Aetheric currently, but they still have physical remnants in what we call – Middle Earth.

We have a lot of evolutionary healing instilled in us to correct the inherent instability we inherited from our Earth. Our Earth's mother

71

accepted us and created fertile lands with feeds of grain and vegetables. Once we, as a planet, have all become vegan, Gaia will open to her divinity and her grace the secrets of the universe. Global warming will stop and even repair past damage in our flooded regions. The understanding of physics and higher math will be made open to us all; as this Tattva is paired with Vayu- Air of the airy part of Earth. Mathematics was the first science, and I mentioned that the earliest mathematician had written my knowledge.

One would be able to stabilize their minds and think more logically if they can meditate on the Tattva of a yellow square in a larger yellow square with a purple frame. Logic and reason will come to the practitioner. If one is confused and cannot even trust their own minds, meditate on its image for a few days and chant PrithviPrithvi several times until your mind settles into focus. A brown or white candle may be helpful with sandalwood incense with a bell to open and close the ritual. A quartz crystal for mediation is a perfect way to tap into this Tattva. A physical image to represent this Tattva would be a mountain.

You might be wondering why the OM symbol uses the water sign so much in all these chakra symbols. The reason for this lies in the mysteries of Water. The original OM did not use the water element at all but uses Akasha. However, Akasha and Apas – Water does have a sustaining influence on overall life. All was made manifest at the same time anyway, so it doesn't matter if Apas was present in the original OM.

The water element houses LIFE itself and all of its mysteries of God. God and life go hand and hand. We need God in the water elements to guarantee that we are alive. If what we call God might not be in the water element, there would be given no reason or logic to life itself. This is the divine baptism. God blessed us will His logic and

73

memories of the divine for us to instill order and reason. We call this order – the Holy Spirit, and it is always accompanied by water, as in baptism. You can say that another word or the OM is the Holy Spirit in Christianity. God is with all souls. Souls are of the water element – Apas.

Earth's element is very dense. We came from a higher vibration only to be lower to come here to manifest God as much as possible in the flesh. We created this universe to do that – to answer our current riddle of - Can we get to know God by trying to manifest Him in the flesh? This is our current challenge. All world spiritualities are far more positive and of a higher mind than to deal with sucha ridiculous riddle. Most spiritual sources will teach you to exit this universe employing your inner peace with God. However, we committed to be here and finish as much as possible of trying to be God in the flesh – the riddle. That is why we have our movie stars, great leaders of fame, great artists, and singing talents of the day – All for just one reason – to manifest God in the flesh. Then we have our world spiritualities to help us to exit it all and be at one with our source – God. You might wonder why talking about God is seen as controversial; this is because the riddle won't be answered if so. Our riddle is anti-God because we must be God ourselves. The workplace can be an evil place; try not to mention God or religion there.

The seven-chakra system

• The *root* chakra comprises of whatever grounds you, for your stability in life. This includes your basic food, water, shelter, and safety. This Chakra helps in letting go of fear. We see the OM in a square with a downward triangle, it is attached to Prithvi Prithvi.

• *Svadhisthana* is the second primary Chakra according to Hindu Tantrism. This Chakra is said to be blocked by fear, especially the fear of

75

death. Opening this Chakra can boost creativity, manifest desire, and help gain confidence. Its symbol is orange with the white crescent moon – it's attuned to Prithvi Apas.

• The Navel Chakra is associated with *Manipura*, the center of personal power and our inner fire. When this Chakra is balanced, self-esteem and confidence are high. It is yellow with an OM and a downward triangle. Some show the Sun symbol with it as well. This Chakra is attuned to Prithvi Agni.

• The fourth Chakra, or Heart Chakra (Sanskrit: *Anāhata*, in English: "unbeaten"), is located at the lower center of the chest. Its primary color is green, most associated with the air element. Anahata is all about love and the flow and exchange of emotional sharing between us and among all living things. Prithvi Vayu, or the airy part of Earth is attuned here. This Chakra connects our physical body to our soul.

76

- Our throat chakra (***Vishuddha***) is connected to our ability to communicate and speak our inner truth. It is blue with a downward water triangle, with a circle and OM in the center. It is attuned to the airy part of water Apas Vayu and is no longer in the Prithvi family of Tattva. Here is where the mysteries of the water element start to make it conscious. The moon card in the tarot deck is represented here. The ruling God here is the Great Lord Vishnu. He is needed to bring clarity to the deep mysteries of the subconscious mind. I hold a more positive view of the moon card than most do. The card represents mysteriously intuitive communications between people, and can be open to angelic influence. Singing in a choir is a good way of attuning this Chakra and speaking the truth from your heart.

- ***Ajna*** is the Chakra of intuition, self-realization, inspiration, and imagination. The energy of this Chakra allows us to see and understand the inner and outer worlds. Ajna is known in the West as the *third eye.* We are granted, clairvoyants. ESP and all psychic visions are through this Chakra. It was two main peddles with an OM in the middle. Our spirit uses this Chakra to guide us to higher realities in life.

• What does the Crown Chakra do? – ***Sahasrara*** - Great sound. This incredible sound is the OM; this Chakra is about spiritual connection and transformation. It lifts and inspires you, connecting you to the divine (you might call this divine energy, the Source, or God). This Chakra also gives you a sense of your divinity, the awareness that you are a soul in a human body. This Chakra has one thousand pedals and connects our physical body and spirit.

Prithvi-Prithvi or the Earthly part of Earth

We can use the image of the yellow square with a purple frame with a smaller yellow square in the center in making this image. The first thing we might ask ourselves is: why so much purple with that little yellow square? The reason is that we are referring to focusing our minds – the mind is usually seen as yellow/purple. I read earlier that all our so-called reality is a mere false dream we are experiencing. All the time is happening simultaneously around us; and reality is relative to the mind and is projected outward from it.

These Tattva are supposed to heal the many corrections in the cosmic soup of chaos. They are designed for balancing and modifications; not just stated as universal principles. Here in Prithvi of Prithvi, the order in chaos is achieved. The tool we use is a clear and focused mind. The Egyptian God Tahiti's wisdom chant is *Anug Hung*. His priests used that chat in their religious works as it was expected of them to have the intelligence needed to address and resolve the problems given to them.

A good diet is needed as well. Avoid alcohol, sweets, and drugs. They say artificial sweeteners are worse than sugar. Get a whole night's rest and exercise. Sunbathing for 15 minutes daily is excellent for the entire body and mind but use sun block. I once acquired a face full of sunspots living across from a beach in Miami. It took a bit to lose them all.

Suppose you practice the rituals using the two meditations I wrote earlier and apply practical thinking and mental clarity. In that case, your mind will clear up over time if dedicatedly applied to the ritual. Use this ritual/meditation if our life has become chaotic and out of focus. Try not to take too much companionship with friends and family; instead, be dedicated to the practice alone, and chant Prithvi-Prithvi with a yellow candle and the square either carved into it or painted on the glass. Use sandalwood incense with a small bowl of salt. The Earth element is the air element forced down by fire and water to make its supreme reality for us. I say now – living in the truth is also needed. One must be very honest with who they are and honest with others – live the fact that you are. Spiritual practice might also be helpful, like yoga or meditation. Remember, a clear mind is a simple mind. They say: Just be true to yourself, and all happiness will be blessed.

More abstract spiritual knowledge will make us quite spacey. The best knowledge is practical knowledge. You want to be grounded in the self with the simplicity of character that people like the most. Working too many hours and being too busy are just the cowards' ways to avoid getting to know who we are. This ritual will also sharpen our intellect, so finer people and money will come into our lives.

Apart from magic, meditation, and a rigorous yoga routine, your daily work will be your best meditation. In Miami, I attended the all-male nude yoga, which was non-sexual. I was so exhausted at the end; I fell asleep on my mat. Miami even has coed naked yoga with a room temperature like a sauna. After a few minutes, one forgets about the nudity and focuses on the yoga asanas alone. I considered this yoga one day for myself. A lot of unhappiness is due to stress and a boring routine, and a good stretch of the muscles might be needed to release negative energies.

There are two organizations: Scientology and the Landmark Forum, which help one get deeper in touch with their subconscious mind. The forum is just a $400 two-day weekend with the following courses that are an option. Scientology sells pricey systems with higher-rated results promised. For both organizations, one must be watchful of spending and only choose paths they feel intuitively right for them. Do your studies on those courses without a high-pressure salesperson involved. Make them work for you without supporting them too much. Apart from them, knowing ourselves deep down is very grounding for our souls.

One advantage that we have over most alien brothers and sisters on their respective planets, is that we have chosen not to live our personal lives in a set, predicted, planned-out manner. In most alien cultures, all aspects of life are arranged for them. Aliens have no personal friendships at all but professional ones only. They make it impossible to get to know each other. Their metaphysics and spirituality, with their highly developed concept of who God is, might tempt us; but as humans on planet Earth, our destiny is meant to overshadow them by far, in due time.

Still, those aliens will only need to reflect on their personalities. If they know themselves and have the personal skills of introspectiveness, they

83

might be like us here on Earth. However, we humans have chosen not to be that way, even if it may hold us back for a while; in the long run, we will finish better.

Instead of this statement, positive inner personal relationships are a sign of higher intellect, another word for maturity.

To set up a Prithvi-Prithvi altar, one needs a yellow cloth, a yellow candle, a statute of Vishnu with his main chant to open the space which is Shri Vishnu Mantra:

त्वमेवमाताचपितात्वमेवत्वमेवबन्धुश्चसखात्वमेव ।
त्वमेवविद्याद्रविणम्त्वमेवत्वमेवसर्वम्ममदेवदेव ॥

Tvameva Maataa Ca Pitaa Tvameva Tvameva
Bandhush-Ca Sakhaa Tvam-Eva.

This is a powerful chant that will open all five Prithvi Tattva with your Prithvi candle:

1.   Have a small bowl of salt and a cup of water with freshly cut greens on a dish.

2.   Use a yellow marker to draw a square on the glass.

3.   Chant 'Prithvi Prithvi' four times.

4.   Address the altar twice a day until the candle burns out.

The unique zodiac sign of this Tattva is Taurus.

The earthy part of Earth is the Earth itself – with all its soil, grasslands, desert, oceans, beaches, and mountains. It is also other planets in our solar system and beyond. One can transport themselves anywhere on our planet if they understand this Tattva well. Location is an illusion. We are everywhere simultaneously; our human egos limit our views to one location and time. The ego does this so we can focus on our life's lessons better.

Yes, some space out and are in multiple locations simultaneously. I used to be very bad like that, and still am sometimes, if my sugar intake is too much. It is a characteristic of my autism that I had to live with most of my life. This autism has cleared up in my mid 40s a great deal, I am glad to say.

What we call topsoil is a true blessing and wonder. This topsoil can grow anything for humanity. Keeping a good compost pit is the key to good gardening. I live in New Orleans, which was a big swamp at one time. Once they drained the swamp in the early 1900s, they put subsoil over it to build up the land. Gardening is impossible with this subsoil. I had to give up. New Jersey was the opposite – anything grows in Jersey! One needs a few hundred or thousand years of grasslands to create good topsoil. The grassland of the mid-west plains of this country – the U.S. – has shallowroots. A good storm can lift the soil. Farming is a skill.

Farms nowadays do use fertilizer that bombs can be made from. I really wonder about our factory farms if the food is right for us or not. We even have biogenetic foods. It is a given skill and blessing of the third Dimension of hybridizing new foods from other plants. Mainly all our vegetables and fruits have been hybridized by man. Both wheat and corn were our first accomplishments, between 50,000 and 12,000 BCE. From there, we could rely on our farming to support a large population. The world's first cities in 12,000 BCE were situated around this farm.

Çatalhöyük in southern Anatolia was one of the earliest cities in the rear east from as early as 12,000 to 10,000 BC but confirmed from 7500 BC to 5,200 BC with a population of 10,000. They farmed, kept life stock, and hunted game. Then, in 7500 BC we had Eridu, Uruk, and Ur in present day Iraq – Mesopotamia.

The Samarra culture dates from 5,500 to 4,800 BC. They were the first culture to use mudbricks and pottery. Before them, the walls were of hay and mud. This new building style allowed them to construct substantial buildings. The pottery allowed the Samarrans to use wine, honey, and milk and trade them with their neighbor. After this culture, the Babylonians took root in the Mesopotamian valley.

The earthly part of the Earth is where energy is most dense. Energy and matter are the same but expressed in two different ways. $e = mc^2$ is what Albert Einstein realized over 100 years ago. Where we were before, in our *in-between lives*, was primarily based on energy with applications of matter. Now we are in an environment with mostly matter but with energy applications. Einstein is wrong in saying that the two are equal when in our case, our realm holds matter acting as energy.

We still need to come up with the right physics between the realms. The day will come when we can explain a lot more than we know now – we are still in the dark regarding other realms. One day, we will be able to understand physics on a multi-realm basis and understand our universe in its entirety much better than we know now. Do not worry; science will progress in due time. The future will be a wonderful place to be in. We are still in the dark about many things currently. Trust me!

To conclude with this Tattva, I say it may serve as a foundation for the rest of the Tattva in the Prithvi series. Try to master it if you can. Try to get involved in the physical Earth if you can help with gardening and landscaping. Try to enjoy the beach, skiing, or a mountain hike, or go on a desert winter hiking trip. Quite a few have died hiking in the summer months around Las Vegas, you know – only hike there in the winter months, I advise you.

Remember the chant *Tvameva Maataa Ca Pitaa Tvameva Tvameva Bandhush-Ca Sakhaa Tvam-Eva*, along with the simple chant of *Prithvi Prithvi* throughout the day.

Prithvi Apas or
the watery part of Earth

Yes, the Earth Plane is finally receiving the rain it badly needs. Now our crops will grow; we will have a fine harvest. However, too much rain has detrimental effects just the same. The symbol of the Tattva is the same as the first, but instead of the small yellow square, we have the white crescent moon representing the water element. One would need their quartz crystal, but better yet, a rose quartz crystal. A yellow candle and patchouli incense would be helpful. You may go to a koi pond or meditation pond with your rose quartz to fertilize your dry mind that is bored of life. They say an empty mind only causes trouble.

Chant *Prithvi Apas* several times by a mediation pond with one's mind full of ideas to keep their very business, and it will leave one quite happy, and much easier to get along. Going to the ocean to view and hear the waves will do the same.

Our problems will wash away. My last property had an ocean view. I enjoyed it for seven years but had to move out because the ocean was too much for me.

You can even do magic with this Tattva. Lay out a purple table cover with a yellow candle on it. With a yellow marker, draw a yellow square on its candle glass, and with a blue marker, draw a white crescent in the center of that. Do that chant four times a day, twice a day, until the candle burns out.

In my lifetime, I have met those who wanted to have me conform to their standards with their efforts to dominate me. I used to play along with their games out of fear of being alone. Now, I like being alone; and I welcome very few people into my private life. Many people wanted me to fear them. I just placated their egos to keep the peace. Many tried to be my teachers; I let them think they were, by allowing them to have the last word to keep the peace. I even used to know a teacher in an Egyptian lodge who believes himself, to this day, to be the Egyptian God – Osiris!

This Egyptian summed it up nicely in his behavior, as he is obviously a self-deluded teacher. I mentioned him because he fills his emptiness with a false sense of having a fantastical identity. He is just fearful of being a nobody! My final word on this meditation is that solitude is divinely beautiful. Just be yourself – do not get lost in fantasy. If you feel that you need to be a famous actor or singer, if it is meant to be, it will happen. Otherwise, just enjoy the trip there. I met so many junior actors who love the process of getting famous alone apart from getting there. In many of these fantasy careers, the process and not the goal is the joy of it.

Some people are empty and shallow, which makes them intolerable to be around. They do not trust anyone to love them; this is a much harder mediation as it takes the Soul into play – the crescent mood. Our subconscious minds are under the moon's influence, which can be irrational and unpredictable. For shallow-minded people, isolation and actively working on the self are needed; either left-minded or right-minded studies might suit one. These people are afraid to be alone, as it might cause them to question who they are and what their life's purpose might be. These people are like human animals who want to go through a predicted way of living set forth by others, omitting their unique individual gift to bear to humanity. Accepting solitude can be scary until we find our inner resources. I say, *"Life is something we must get through and not reinvent every occasion."*

Being too socially minded to the point of conformity will only ruin us. God is within us all. How we experience God is our inward religion. Any of God's so-called days of Judgment, are death and renewal to a higher way to live — and not death at all; moreover, we must gain a greater sense of life itself. Man created both death and any books called

94

the words of God. God is not the author of either of them.

Now, on the good side of this Tattva, the Earth is made fertile. When the nation of Israel was established on May 14, 1948, upon the arrival of Jewish immigrants from Europe and Russia, their government plan was to irrigate large areas of land for farming and livestock to support its newly growing population. Deserts were turned green all over Israel. Likewise, in the American Southwest, pot farming provides food for that region of the country.

On a personal level, a good job will bring fertility to your life. A special dinner to celebrate love brings water to your desert of the heart. It is essential to be noticed in a relationship; take the lead and arrange a dinner for the two of you. Having friends and family over will moisten your soil. If you are lonely during the holidays, try to be with at least one other person or volunteer for the church Christmas party.

I make a book recommendation that aligns with the healing and balancing of this Tattva, which is Thomas Moore's book, *The Care of the Soul.* Thomas Moore's *Care of the Soul* poses an adventuresome meditation upon the sacred art of soulful living in his book. A program for bringing the Soul back to life. What does Moore mean by Soul? He writes: *"Soul is not a thing but a quality or Dimension of experiencing life and ourselves. It involves: depth, value, relatedness, heart, and personal substance."*

For him, the Soul is the seat of emotions and the hub of our lives. Moore claims that a loss of Soul lies behind many contemporary men and women's restlessness, addiction, insecurity, and frustration. With lives devoid of meaning and purpose, people yearn for drugs and drinking to nourish their souls. Thomas Moore's explanation can be applied to the need for intimate relationships or the solo path of the artist. For the most part, we have the low road – relationships; in that most people choose personal relationships to satisfy the Soul's needs. However, one can only take this path for so long until one must take the artist's solo path as the high road.

I recommend Thomas Moore for providing a recipe for soulful living in troubled times. He helps us see that we can survive and learn from our troubles, tragedies, and follies. And by challenging us to care for our souls, Moore draws a picture of the bounties of spirituality. Ultimately, he calls us to our true vocation, which is to care for the world's Soul and celebrate the sacred arts of life. *Care of the Soul* is an essential primer for those who want to relate spirituality to everyday life.

So, the crescent moon in this Tattva may also represent the Soul. The Soul needs contact with the Earth Plane. The water element rules the Soul. Between the two, we can see the nourishing mother

97

trying to care for her young and to make everything memorable. However, it starts with us only inviting those to enter our lives, who are at peace with themselves. I say, "if you want to be respected, be respectful of others first." In business, they say that *you are protected by professional behavior.* If we are a victim of evil behavior, just holdfast and do not react to them; in time, they will all be exposed for who they are – bad!

The image for this Tattva is mud. In mud, everything can grow; you can make pottery and bricks for building homes. Without the water on Earth, our planet would not be able to maintain life here. Water is the psyche of humanity as well. Our psyche has demanded that we need a planet with over seventy percent ocean coverage.

Eighty percent of our world's oxygen comes from our oceans and twenty percent from our forests. Deforestation is terrible for our environment as less carbon dioxide is taken from the air; this only adds to the greenhouse warming of our planet. I read somewhere that global warming is proper for our world to warm up, and we are helping it alone. They say that we might even be heading to another ice age.

My counsel for you now is to drink enough water throughout the day to rid your body of impurities and awaken your body to the water (Apas) element in Prithvi.

All life seems to grow when water touches the parched Earth. Awaken yourselves to a new future of the splendor of God's majesty and reinstate in full the promise for a new tomorrow by opening to the waters of life.

Prithvi Agni or
the Fiery part of Earth

The Tattva symbol here is like the others, but instead of a crescent moon with its yellow square, we have a red upward triangle as the fire element on Earth. The name *Agni* comes from Sanskrit, meaning **"fire,"** and the Tattva system. It expresses itself as **"truth,"** **"reality,"** or **"thatness."** Agni is also the name of the Hindu god of fire. We see that the God Agni rules along with Vishnu in this Tattva.

One fact to note here, is that Vishnu leads the divine while Shiva is the physical. However, Vishnu service is required to heal a vulnerable element like Prithvi. We could add a Shiva statue to our lower element alters arrangements equally. Now, do you see why Vishnu rules here? It's not because that is his elements − when, in fact, it's Shiva's element; it's because Vishnu is needed to heal a troubled element such as the Prithvi − earth element.

In the Tarot card system, the tower represents itself here. Defending our rights and not being abused are managed here. Being over-defensive and arrogant is just immaturity and small-mindedness. Some people say that a good fight clears the air. However, if it is only a release of negative emotions, it can be seen as abusive behavior. There must be truth to the surface to have a *fair fight.* One must stick to the facts rather than just how they affect them. Compromising is essential in relationships. Over-defensiveness is just a selfish and insecure way of thinking. Being realistic about one's demands will offer little stress in our resolutions.

Having the last word is just small-minded arrogance, and is abusive and counterproductive in relationships. We must speak to others how we care to be spoken to; otherwise, such anti-social skills will only work against us in the long run. Social skills are valuable tools to acquire in life. Social

101

skills must be used in negotiating our interests with others.

We see a volcano shooting up new earth matter between the two to build our planet. The idea of cardinal Earth comes into play here, like the zodiac sign of Capricorn. Career, duty, and reputation come to play here. The Tattvartha or consciousness of the Tattva is first seen in this Tattva. The **'thatness'** is what is in question brought to light by Agni – fire. Fire is the supreme reality test in the Tattva system, while water (Apas) represents illusions and misunderstanding of life.

We see a new Earth forming with a new ground of operation. A new footing on new soil is here for new fertile growth. When Europeans arrived in the new world, they exploited it for what it had. They later took advantage of its land values. Contemporary societies were formed. The English, French, Portuguese, and Spanish spread their culture into this new world. The Italians were

102

satisfied with their spice trade with India to finance colonies in the new world; otherwise, the Germans had no interest but to later immigrate in high numbers making them the most significant minority in the USA. The largest minority in Argentina are the Italians, with many Italians in the Empire states of the USA.

The concept of new opportunity comes into play here in this Tattva of growth. They say that newly formed land after a lava flow is the best for farming in Hawaii. Earthly fertility and prosperity are the gifts of this Tattva. So, if you need new opportunities in business, do a meditation upon Tattva with a yellow or brown candle with cinnamon oil around it; with a red upward triangle marked on the candle glass on a Tuesday, Thursday, or Sunday. Light Acacia incense, and invoke the energies of the Tattva twice a day, until the flame is out. A Vishnu, Shiva, and Agni statue is also suitable for our Agni altar.

103

The spirit of the Tattva will come when it feels ready to help you. Agni is the soul reflection of Akasha, and offers a firsthand witness to Akasha through Agni; this Tattva will implant ideas in your intuition and dream times. Earth elementals are very loyal and can make lifelong friends. You might even be invited to a house brownie as the Prithvi spirits are brownies – you know? Never make an offering of food and water to them. They will take from your food and drinks as they please. However, one quartz crystal might make a home for them that would be acceptable. The unique zodiac sign to this Tattva is Capricorn: emphasizing career and reputation.

An image of new lava flow might serve as a visual image for Prithvi Agni, the fiery part of Earth. The goddess Pele with her Hawaiian island's religious practice now called Huna, which means - secret, might help work with this Tattva. This new-aged faith, Huna, is different from the authentic ancient worship of the Hawaiian Islands. It was designed by a white American to sell his books and workshops, though it offers an extensive view into Hawaiian worship, if not the authentic worship itself now. We cannot throw gorgeous women and girly-like men into an active Volcano nowadays – now, can we?

The heating up of our foods uses this element as our foods are Prithvi; the heating or cooking part is Agni; we thus have food preparations as we know them today. Using fire to cook food is an ancient practice dating back at least two million years. Archaeologists have found evidence that Paleolithic humans used fires to roast meat and cook vegetables centuries earlier than was previously believed.

Hot spices are used to prepare early man's food from ancient India. According to historians, some of the earliest applications of spices were probably as preservatives, or as a means of disguising spoilt meat while transporting it over

105

long distances. Some historians believe that the first spiced dishes were accidentally created when cooks stored meat in containers with certain types of peppers.

The fiery parts of Earth can even have significant earthquakes. Our Earth's mantle moves with its inner river of lava around the inner Earth. The fact is: our planet is very much like the fiery part of Earth. Our core is made up of iron and nickel, with molding silicon and cobalt over that, with a volcanic glass near the surface that we call lava.

Our planet will never freeze as Mars did, over a billion years ago. Mars used to maintain life back then when our world was not ready. Several billion years ago, the planet Venus used to be lush and green. However, the surface of the Sun grew and heated up that world to a fiery hell as we see it today. I have read that the Master Jesus had evolved on the planet Venus eons ago. One day our own planet will heat up as Venus did. We might have to colonize Mars or find a suitable planet like ours. A year ago, I had a dream telling me that a double of our planet is ready for us to colonize. I recall in the dream that a famous comedian wasn't laughing. I took this to mean that the dream was serious and that an earth double is waiting for us to colonize one day in our future. We would probably need to discover wormhole travel to get there, as the distance is unreasonably long to travel conventionally.

You might ask: what does this mean to me? The answer is that in our crisis (Agni), we find a better way to live. So, Agni – fire can mean disaster if we are living falsely. Agni is the supreme reality of life, the first manifestation of Akasha – a universal truth. Agni is our earthly local truth and is not universal but a fragment of the whole of a universal truth unknown to humanity. So, the fiery part of Earth is a local truth fitting for humanity's needs, like a guiding light to show us our enlightenment here. The archetype of the Devil in hell is our savior as it frees us from the old and false ways of living. In the bible, the Devil is seen as a servant of God. It is best to make friends with this Devil and work with him to get yourself out of the hell fires of life. What they mean by the saying: "You must get to know the Devil by his name", is that in order to know if it's good or bad for you, you must try it and experience it firsthand. This is the basis of the reason why we have evil in our world.

Evil consists of both being stupid and immature. We experience the evil of it in an odd attempt at gaining knowledge and maturity. As you can see, all behavior is an attempt at good and bad growth. We experience the bad of it when we approach gaining knowledge and maturity in the wrong way. However, we eventually get it right in the long run.

One usually thinks of a volcano when thinking about this Tattva. A volcano brings up new

108

fertile Earth for framing. The new hardened lava is perfectly fine to grow anything. Life seems to take root easily on this new Earth. So, with you using this Tattva magic, you will have new fertile opportunities. Just lay out your purple tablecloth with a yellow candle in glass on it. Draw with a yellow marker, a yellow square and a red upward triangle in the center. Then chant *Prithvi Agni* twice daily, until the candle flame burns out.

Prithvi Vayu or
the Airy part of Earth

The airy part of Earth uses the same yellow field with a purple frame, but we have a blue circle in its center. The blue circle of Vayu is the air influence in this Tattva. The physical image of this Tattva is the waves of sand in a desert. The unique astrological zodiac sign of Tattva is Virgo.

When we have Vayu present, it brings awareness of any Tattva houses. What we have here is an awareness of our resources, and the awareness of our responsibilities, service, and debt. We might be overlooking this in our life crises - the solution is at hand. If we are having problems seeing it, the Tattva magic/mediation consciousness might change to the Prithvi Agni for you to know the answer to your crisis better than Prithvi Vayu.

The energies will change again to Prithvi Vayu upon you spotting the problem; and further analyses will occur in the airy part of Earth. You, however, may be invoking the wrong forces to begin with. The Tattva collective whole will guide you to the right magic to help yourself in your unique crisis.

Studiousness and analysis are instilled here in our aid. It just might be evident that we are overlooking this unknowingly to us. Aiming for perfection is fostered in this Tattva. The Tattva will raise your standards for your project. If it is art, your art will be perfect; if math, it will all be correct.

The Vayu is Blue because it is purely a Krishna and Brahman energy. There is no lie and delusion to your magic with this Tattva, or they will bring bad luck and sadness to your life. The blue circle of Krishna will help you in your discernment in solving your problems here. A Krishna statue with an offering will be helpful here as the correct viewing of the problem is half the problem solved.

Brahman – the supreme godhead of man indicates the absolute reality of the Universe. Many religions try to depict such a paradise in various realms of Earth and Spirit. We seem to know that this is our goal. Such a perfect setting for us can be achieved if we meditate and do our magic with this Tattva.

If you work with this Tattva, a visceral awareness of the truth will awaken your nerves. You will get this awareness about people, places, and things. You will even be aware of what country you had your last incarnation in, and who you were in that life. Also, an awareness of opportunities unknown to you will submerge in the period of our invocation of the energies.

Since Virgo rules this Tattva, living in the present is a gift to reap when working with it. Being practical-minded and grounded, I associated it with all Prithvi Tattva. With Vayu involved, you gain conscious awareness of such groundings. You know how to work hard and get along with your work partners; you know what is essential, and you do not like gossip or start trouble with others. Your head is full of critical things to think about; you can even use Prithvi Vayu magic for a troublemaking friend who can only gossip and instigate trouble with others.

To prepare your Prithvi Vayu altar, put down yellow and blue cloth with a tall yellow candle in glass. Upon it, draw in blue ink a circle - light sandalwood or Pine incense with some Krishna, Brahman, or Vishnu with offers would be helpful. Chant Prithvi Vayu four times, twice daily, in front of your altar.

What Vayu gives to Prithvi is that it reflects the universal vibration wonderfully. Vayu is consciousness serves as the consciousness of Prithvi – Earth, Gaia, our Earth Mother. The consciousness of the Earth is knowledge from our Earth's mother. If we can attune our minds to this Tattva, Gaia can

113

open her secrets to us early. There are people in the New Age movement, and the Dali Lama who has some insights into her wisdom. Understanding the universal brotherhood will also be open to us in that case. The government of Shambhala might be able to use us as one of its Illuminati if our attunements are right. I feel that I was used to heralding the fall of the Berlin Wall five years before it fell just by predicting its fall. I was never used again, but I hope it will be in the future as an Illuminati. Some Illuminati are only used once, as I was in the summer of 1984.

Remember, with Vayu, all righteousness needs to be upheld with proper behavior and speech. Under its influence, you might be attracted to churches or Temples to be at one with the refined energies there. To visualize your success, you might feel at home with your quartz crystals by creating an altar with them. What we are talking about is the spiritualization of your environment. Under its influence, your house or apartment will be extra clean and fresh smelling. Your cat litter will be clean with no odors. The front of your home will also be well-presented to the neighborhood. You will bathe and brush your teeth daily under the influence of Prithvi Vayu.

The elemental life forms called Brownie will direct you in all these facets of improvement. The ones in this Tattva will only work with you if your house is clean and you wash regularly enough. Your bedding must be clean and fresh before they can enter your home to work with you, or else they will do nothing for you.

I have a spirit guide named – Spartacus. He can forcefully and quickly get the wrong people out of my house. He can come to me in a time of great need. Spartacus can be punitive and swift in protecting me in my house. Now, he is helping me to move to South Florida. Here in New Orleans, it is getting far too violent, with drug gang wars in the

115

crossfire in my neighborhood these days. I also have a house brownie named – lik lik. He blessed my house with many columns of energy for my own good. He said he would also protect my house from a deadly hurricane.

So, we can consciously look into Prithvi to see exactly what it is. The most important thing we can see is opportunities here on Earth. Our first gift from Prithvi was obtaining a human body with a family to raise us. We should be glad that we live in these times where education is encouraged. There were times when education could only be found in monasteries before the Age of Enlightenment in the 1800s. Back then, noble families sent their youth to monasteries to achieve a primary education, sophisticated wordly knowledge, and learning commerce.

The appreciation of education and self-studies is noticed, given this Tattva. The age of Aquarius dawned in the 1800s when the industrial revolution was in full swing. Public school was open free of charge to all children of any class ranking. People have not been relying on their religions to teach them how to view God as how they did in the age of Pisces. People want to know God for themselves firsthand, and not be taught faith from a set body of beliefs set out from them.

Working hard in a focused manner can be taught under the tutelage of this Tattva. We could take advantage of every opportunity handed to us. We could make the most out of them all and succeed in life.

Matter does have consciousness. Meditating with quartz crystals or having many around your house will awaken you to the divinity of the Earth element. They say that quartz crystal is attuned to 32768Hz. The universal is attuned to 432 Hz; this is equal in Hz to - Agni, which is a local soul truth of Akasha - Vayu also is a universal truth of 432 HZ that mirrors Akasha in its reflection. Agni reflects

117

Akasha on a local soul level upon the Earth, 432Hz. So, Agni is at 432Hz. This fact makes our planet Earth a fine place to gain universal awareness. Now we have Bruce Cathie's figure of 144,000 minutes of arc per second for the speed of light. 144.000 minutes of arc equals 6.66 revolutions of the Earth! We can see two numbers sacred in the Holy Bible here - what does that mean? Some even call the 144,000 Hz the God Hertz or the touch of God in our Universe. What do you think?

Many minerals have their unique vibration signature to attune up to our awakening. You can even go to Sedona, Arizona, to bathe in the Earth's energies, a mixture of Prithvi. Apas, Agni and Vayu. I found the most Earth Vortexes in New York City than anywhere. I even have my private vortex in West 23rd St by a big tree. Only my friend Kim and I know of it. Sedona, Arizona, has quite a few of these vortexes. I have been there twice and hope to retire there one day. A vortex is when we have a

118

dimple between the seven levels of our Earth's realms. Cosmic energies pass through the vortexes to bless all of humanity. They specially bless those who meditate around its energies. At Sedona, they have male, female, and neutral vortexes. They say Mount Shasta has a strong vortex and serves as the root chakra of the planet.

In Mulaprakriti, I mean to say the mother of all four Tattva – Prithvi, Apas, Agni, and Vayu. The magic that creates sweet atoms in Earth Planes comes from this soup's origin in Mulaprakriti. In this universally blessed way, we can experience a universal sense of joy in the physical; this shows that our physical planes were no accident; they were meant to be and are blessed as divine.

Apas, Agni, and Vayu are not as divine as Prithvi – the Earth Planes are. I had read about very high angels who are way higher than the Earth's Plane level and have lost their physical bodies and put their noses up to physical plane incarnations to revitalize their Aetheric Bodies. They do not realize that their time is limited. A material embodiment is required for their vitality.

I read that if they refuse to incarnate to serve in a low physical world as a savior, others will be forced in due time. Those great angels will need to rebuild their physical bodies again, which can start in the animal kingdom, then be an unevolved human to a highly evolved human to be ready to be such a savior for a dark world in need of a savior. Christ and Buddha came to us in our hour of need – they were not forced!

Sweet atoms are only seen in the Prithvi planes as universal energies feed for the soul who incarnates here. Yes, we have Apas Akasha, and there is a feeding of the sweet atom there, too; however, the energies are singular to the water element. Upon the physical planes, all four elements create an excellent soup of sweet atoms that feed the soul for their growth instead of simply sustaining one in the astral planes with the Apas Akasha's sweet atoms. I first brought up the topic of sweet atoms in my second book – Personal growth in the multi-Dimensional Multiverse, in 2021 when I was writing the book in New Orleans, Louisiana, USA.

The astral plane is of a watery element, so sweet atoms are only present in its mixture with

123

Prithvi, which offers its form for living there. As a result, it can sustain a soul but not for long- an earthly incarnation would be needed in due time.

So, the Akasha in Prithvi brings us great joy. One way to invoke its energies is through the Agni element of fire. Take at least twenty minutes of sunlight and drink water set in the sunlight for over a day in a large plastic or glass jug. It would be finer if you could add a few quartz crystals to the sunshine water. Drink at least four tall glasses of it per day. You will be polarized between the two with the Sun's - Agni fire element.

The Vayu Tattva is unique because it reflects the mother of the four elements like a mirror. It does so on a conscious level. Keeping your house, teeth, and body clean can bring Akasha to enlighten your home with universal joy. Taking up a spiritual path is far better than the path of drugs, gambling, or alcohol.

124

Self-education utilizing my automatic writing is my spiritual path currently. However, it will change to meditation when Neptune reaches Aries in March 2025. I will be learning Kundalini Yoga by then. I will be so glad to get out of my head and into my body finally—I am looking forward to it, I must say. I wish to learn levitation as well with my meditations. I also hope to work as an actor by then when I return to South Florida.

Working on your creativity will bring Akasha into the physical. The arts, dance, acting, sculpting in clay or stone, drawing, composing music, and playing an instrument can bring universal joy to the physical. I enjoy composing for the Harp, Violin, and Piano in my shared time and book writing.

To perform Prithvi Akasha magic meditations, you set up your altar like the other four, but draw a purple egg on the glass-covered candle. Use Bois descends - Sahara Noir is fine but a bit too airy; it smells mostly of frankincense without the

125

baggage of amber, smoke, or wood. Or you can use frankincense incense. Place a few large quartz crystals upon your altar with water, salt, and perhaps a little honey as an offering to Lord Brahman. Chant *Prithvi Akasha* four times per sitting twice daily until your candle is burned out. Consider letting universal joy into your life, everyone around you, and the world.

Eating organic foods in season that are locally grown is essential for Akasha to inhabit your body. You are, in fact, your local area's energy, and it is critical to buy local farmers' market-grown foods as much as possible. Go to your local dairy farm and buy their milk, cheese, and butter. Go to town farmers' markets and buy as many locally grown foods as possible.

People in the eastern European Slavic nation of Georgia live so long because they eat locally grown organic foods. Their average life span is around 110 years old to 130 at the most. These

126

people are full of Akasha and rarely get sick. Some move outside of their country, and they get sick quite often. There is no processed food with preservatives in the Slavic nation of Georgia.

Most of all, we need to have Akasha in us, be positive and forgive others for being weak in heart toward us. Pray for world peace and the liberation of the Ukrainian people. When doing this magic, lay your purple tablecloth on your altar with a yellow candle in its center, draw on the glass of the yellow candle square and a purple teardrop egg in its center, and chant *Prithvi Akasha* four times twice a day until your candle burns out. An image of this Tattva around to remind yourself of your intentions could help.

Pray for world peace and then peace with a return to you. Prayer is like a mirror; what you pray for is what you get; it may be for others or for the world – it returns to you. So, keep your prayer

127

positive always. Then, the blessings will return to you.

Apas–Water

Apas Tattva Water, or the White Crescent Moon in the Night Blue Field

Now we must talk about the mysteries of the Water element. Water was born from Fire to clarify all misunderstandings about the two. In this way, Apas became the opposite of Agni. You might wonder why? The answer lies in our strange world of dualities.

It is an illusion that Apas is different from Agni, when in fact, they are the same element but expressed differently. The other way of view comes when the light of Agni is diffused when it comes from Akasha – supreme truth. Agni is the firstborn from Akasha but created unstable and needs grounding. Apas became unfocused diffusion with a negative polarity to Agni's positive polarity. The two genuinely exist magnetically as two elements with two different expressions of the one element – *Akasha in duality*. Water – Apas being negative

130

while Agni – fire being positive. The two attract each other magnetically but need Prithvi – Earth to focus and stabilize the two.

The results are – Vayu – air or knowledge/ wisdom/ consciousness of the Earth – Prithvi, in respect to the polarity combustion - Fire and water. Vayu is a projection of Prithvi in the form of consciousness and knowledge; these two are considered lower expressions and not divine.

However, we use them to achieve our liberation for Prithvi and the whole of the realms of Maya. Maya seems best in Apas/Prithvi, the lower elements - Shiva. At the same time, the higher elements are attuned to Vishnu, where salvation is needed. Again, I say the Vishnu is attuned to Prithvi solely to uplift and aid it and is not its actual ruler.

The odd environment of this duality is the reason why Agni created Apas. And to it, all its diffusions are embodied in one element – water (Apas); this makes Apas the element of illusions.

You might wonder why our life and our psyche are of this delusive element? That answer lies in our holding to both elements of Agni and Apas together with no special expression in Prithvi or Vayu. Our spirit is stabilized in Agni, and our souls in Apas. The domain of Agni is the seventh to the ninth Dimension, but gives life everywhere just the same, and Apas with all others below it – the sixth Dimension down.

The air element is consciousness, which ends in the thirteen Dimensions. Prithvi is from the second to the eighth Dimension. As you can see, blending opposites can only bring confusion and duality. However, advanced souls understand the two to be just one expression – combustion; or, to say – Lord Krishna. Only in Krishna can the two be understood as one expression: Action.

132

So, why is the human psyche placed under the water element? The reason is to house our misunderstanding about this odd new delusive realm we are in currently. We would be lost here, if not for Agni shining its light of Akasha; this light of Agni – fire which is tailored to our human needs on Earth. Between Agni – the guiding Fire of light, and its parent Akasha, we will find our way to work out our karma (desires) for coming to such an odd existence like the one we are in currently.

As a result of the focus we had applied to Prithvi - Earth, we collectively made and created the air element (consciousness). Without our consciousness that was made manifest in the Vayu – air, the earth element would not function for us on a personal level. Vayu is also the atmosphere we need to breathe. The spirit of life entered Adam's body through the breath. Vayu- air or consciousness is needed for us to know God – or try and solve the riddle of knowing God by trying to be Him?

The first grain of knowledge we obtained was our independence from our source as a free-standing Ego: Agni/ Vayu – fire/air. Our Egos are the identity we have gained in trying to make sense of the confusion we have initiated in coming here. The Ego is an illusion in itself and does not exist in the minds that hold proper understanding of Apas – Water or psyche.

The Prithvi element was created much later in our evolutionary timeline of growth. We did not need it apart from a new way of development involving Prithvi himself. Before then, we existed in heavenly kingdoms with no identity or methods of growing. All growth is associated with Prithvi alone. We had universal spenders to satisfy us all, and we were content with that for the longest time. One thing we were not doing was addressing our initial reason for leaving God's side to be in these factitious realms. Only in the physical realms of

Prithvi were we able to try to manifest God as a God made in the flesh to understand Him better.

You might ask: why is the water element associated with life? We have found Apas to be the closest element we can identify with - even more than the Earth element- Prithvi. That is why our afterlife experience in those magical realms is so water-like. We call them the Astral planes or the star realms of our in-between life experiences kingdoms.

Paramahansa Nandayoga wrote in Autobiography of a Yogi, "*The astral universe . . . is hundreds of times larger than the material universe . . . with many astral planets, teeming with astral beings.*"

This home is where we originated before we decided to take on our growth in a bolder, direct level, of manifesting God and not simply worshipping God; it merely came up that having celestial joy is not all there needs to be in life. This home is in our psyches to ground our duties in the physical planes. In the astral worlds, we were not grounded in manifesting God as we do here. Growth as manifesting God isn't an issue there.

Since we have committed to physical existence, we are at one with it as our source of life – Prithvi – Earth. We need to incarnate in the physical to maintain our presence; or else, we will die as physical souls and have life in the hinter realms, not working upon our duties as manifesting God in the flesh.

According to occult teachings, the astral plane can be visited consciously through astral projection, meditation, mantra, near-death experience, lucid dreaming, or other means. Individuals that are trained in the use of their astral vehicle can separate their consciousness in the astral vehicle from the physical body at will.

136

The first stage in development, according to Ramacharaka, is "mastery of the physical body and its care and attention. This is pertaining not only to the physical body, but also to its double in the astral. In addition, one must spend time tuning the "instinctive mind."

The first three subdivisions of the intuitive mind are passions, desires, and lusts. The second stage is the intellect, otherwise known as the sharpening of the mind. Someone operating primarily out of the intuitive sense would "have only a glimmering of intellect"; therefore, those centered on the intellect would only have an inkling of the spiritual. Once both stages are completed, the spiritual mind can be awakened.

The term "astral" may refer to the Aether in early theosophical literature. Later theosophical authors such as Annie Besant and C. W. Leadbeater make the astral finer than the Aetheric plane but "denser" than the mental plane. An Aetheric Plane

137

was introduced to create a unified view of seven bodies and remove earlier Sanskrit terms. The term "astral body" replaced the former Kama Rupa - sometimes termed the *body of emotion, illusion, or desire*. Some propounding such claims explain their belief that letting go of desires is spiritual progress by noting that the more one lets go of earthly 'desire', or feelings; one would be less tied down to the physical world, a world of illusion – and more connected to the heavenly, where all is visible and known.

According to Max Heindel's Rosicrucian writings, *desire stuff* is a type of force-matter in continuous motion, responsive to the slightest *feeling*. The desired worlds are also said to be the abode of the dead for some time after death. In the higher regions of the desired worlds, thoughts take a definite form and color perceptible to all, all is light, and there is but one long day.

138

He learned from his gurus in his book *Autobiography of a Yogi,* in which *Paramhansa Yoga Nanda* details the astral planes. Yoga Nanda claims that nearly all individuals enter the astral planes after death. There, they work out the seeds of past karma through astral incarnations, or if their karma requires, they return to earthly incarnations for further refinement. Once an individual has attained the meditative state of Nirvikalpa Samadhi in an earthy or astral incarnation, the soul may progress upward to the "illumined astral planet" of Hiranyaloka. After this transitional stage, the soul may move upward to the more subtle causal spheres, where many more incarnations allow them to refine further before the final unification.

Earth is just a mere hut if the village is an astral plane. This Astral home is much livelier and more expansive than the Earth. I say expansions as their expanses upon our earthly experiences only.

Yes, they have schools there to prepare souls for their human incarnations. Live take up an all-new agenda in the astral planes of many worlds. One can experience joy and love there much more than on Earth.

It is hard to write about the astral, apart from saying that it has a water-like nature and is often in flux – only some physical things there are subject to changes. One needs to be in the same state of change and flux as their worlds are to exist there. The one that isn't subject to change is – the personal content of the soul. Who you are inside can never change – the only place it can be changed is on the physical planes here.

In the astral worlds, one is far more aware of the inner mysteries of who they are but with nowhere to validate them but to incarnate the physical planes. One has a series of a group of physical incarnations then they have a very extended stay in the astral worlds to make sense of them all and to expand upon them all.

To perform magic with this Tattva, lay down a night blue tablecloth or navy blue. Place a white candle in glass with a white crescent moon on the altar. Then chant *Apas Apas* four times twice daily until the candle flame burns out.

Pray for good emotional balance in yourself and your friends who are in need. Pray for a robust astral body for Astro-projections so you may travel to the place of needed healing in your life.

Apas Prithvi or the
Earthy part of Water

The earthly part of water's symbol is a white crescent moon in a night blue field with a yellow square in the center of that moon. In nature, its symbol is *ice*, the solid form of water. Prithvi makes solid any element it influences. If all the ice in the world melted, we would have minimal land to live on. Our planet needs to have its ice glaciers.

Water can be seen as a liquid asset, too - cash. When Prithvi – the Earth is involved, we freeze our liquid assists in investments. Frozen assets can grow in the stock market, and if you have a suitable investment - you might get rich! Fixed assets may be in the form of real estate. You can add that to your bank money to your total assets.

Life started to form out of the bottomless oceans. The earliest time for the origin of life on Earth is at least 3.77 billion years ago, and possibly as early as 4.28 billion years ago — not long after the oceans formed 4.5 billion years ago. After the Earth's formation 4.54 billion years ago, life began to evolve in the deep vents under our ancient oceans.

First, single-celled organisms developed and became multi-celled life forms attached to the ocean floor. One day they detached and formed fish of all kinds. Then a fish started to walk upon the land and evolved into the first dinosaurs! Then, after climatic disasters, furry mammals had their chance to develop - then apes to man; as you can see, we became solid from the water element in our forward evolution.

Our next level of evolution will be in outer space in the Akasha element. Who knows how we would look under low gravity in space stations? We will have to create our own gravity in very large space wheels. We would have to grow our food on those wheels in outer space.

143

In an earlier book, *The Enigma of God*, I wrote that our destiny as a planetary race is to colonize space in such large space-wheel environments. Earth's cities will levitate over the planet many feet up in the atmosphere. The Earth will return to its natural beauty apart from some farming upon the Earth's surface. The only planetary communities will be for agricultural interest alone around farms. The fact is – we as life the Apas Prithvi element. The idea of Apas Prithvi is life itself; this Tattva is the foundation of all growth as it represents our human bodies materialized from the nothingness of the water element - Apas.

You might wonder why I mention frozen assets with human evolution in this same chapter. The reason is that the local arm of our galaxy's council had decided many billions of years ago that Human life would pay out as an investment to enrich the local arm of our galaxy with a finer way of living.

In my earlier book, *The Enigma of God*, I also mentioned that we are to process beyond many other angelic races by being human and sticking to earthly incarnations exclusively. Many other life forms find it odd that our race of souls seems to just incarnation exclusively to one planetary system alone. There is a mystery to our world that our Earth's mother cares to share with us herself in due time as we evolve. I wrote earlier that the Earth has the same Hz as the universe; this opens to us, here on Earth, the universe's secrets in one planetary experience instead of traveling over the universe to get the same experience – A universal awareness!

The Astral planes we go to in our in-between lives are very much Apas Prithvi or the earthly part of water. To an Astral entity, their environment feels quite physical. Its central element is water; however, but a physical form of water it is. Our

145

Astrals planes exist far off in the coldness of outer space, far away from planetary life. That is why many who experience in-between lives in regression say they felt far away. These astral planets are a hundred times more numerous than the physical planets in our own universe. I read once from an esoteric source that the Earth is just a small hut to the larger village around it. That shows how populated the Astrals are concerning the physical planets.

I say again that planet Earth represents the mysteries of our whole universe on just one planet – our Earth. Since humans have evolved here, our Earth's mother, Gaia, will personally share these mysteries with us. She did not share them with our parent race – the Elohim, as they originated on a far-off planet. Our Earth's mother could not accept them as her own.

They grew technologically but not as spiritually as we are meant to grow. The Elohim migrated to a lower level of Earth when the planet had frozen many millions of years ago. They terraformed that planet to suit their needs; they will rejoin us and interbreed with us to form one race of humans one day in the future.

Crystallizing the best out of the water element is implied here in this Tattva. If you can use meditation and do this Tattva magic, you can gain the best of the essence of life needed for growth. We feel that we are full of life but quite dry inside. The essence of life itself is a mystery of humanity. Life needs to be unfolded over time. However, one can tap into its secrets by meditating and doing its magic. The results will be beyond words for everyone; its application is entirely personal.

The appreciation of love can be better understood and more loving as the essence of life unfolds to you. If you can do this, you might be very popular amongst your friends and get the job you are interviewing for. You would gain a charismatic

147

nature about yourself as love is a strong force we all need in this hard life.

The Buddha said: *if we could just be kind to each other, 95 percent of all world's evil would be gone.* Evil people have extraordinarily little of life's forces in them. I recall my grandmother, who was growing weaker by the day. Her behavior was horrible as she felt her vital force leaving her body; this opened her up to demonic possessions of her soul. The demons tried to taunt me, but my mother always protected me from her viciousness. She did not know why she had such evil intentions toward me and my family. She eventually got too weak to be malicious then she died.

It shows how important love and life are - truly, they are the same. The mystery of life and love is that you are the other people in another body. Jesus Christ summed it up in his golden rule: *Treat others the same way you want to be treated.* Between what the Buddha and the Lord

Jesus said, our world would be at peace, we would be of one global government, and we would also be vegetarian; this is our next level of growth.

Community help is this Tattva made manifest. It is when love is grounded in institutions like charities, hospitals, and government programs to help those in need. This Tattva is also fair to governments who are not warlike. The nation of Russia, under Putin, is now a threat to democracy and human rights. China's desire to annex Taiwan is another pending threat to world peace. The Muslim nations are at peace now, but for how long - we do not know. We need to pray for peace in Eastern Europe now. Putin needs to be overthrown as president of the Russian Federation to end the unnecessary war in Ukraine.

St Teresa of Lisieux wished not to have her heavenly reward in heaven but to have her heaven here upon the Earth, helping others to love each other better. She was a prime example of Apas Prithvi - love made in the flesh!!

To do this magic/meditation, lie out an orange cloth with a blue candle and a yellow square drawn on its glass. Use sandalwood incense with salt and water in their own cups. Chant *Apas Prithvi* four times twice a day until the seven-day candle in glass has burned out.

Apas Apas or
The Watery Part of Water

The symbol to this Tattva is a night blue field with a white crescent moon in the center with another white crescent moon in that center. Its symbols in nature are honey, sugar, and candy.

The watery part of water is the emotions of the human psyche. These emotions reflect the waters of the psyche in a reactionary manner. We only feel good if we are growing on a particular level or have friends who share the same values and sympathize with us either for the good or bad. The human psyche is based on confusion and is out of focus. If it feels vulnerable, it can retreat into itself and be self-absorbed; which only makes things worse for the soul. Feeling isolated causes one to be apathetic toward others. Feeling misunderstood can cause the soul to attack others or to withdraw from society.

One's special desires are housed in the Apas-water element. In this Tattva of the watery part of water, one can feel the life of each desire we have. Desires have lives of their own, apart from human souls. These desires are water elementals called Sylves. Either these desires are satisfied, or they are changed for a higher one. Desires are eternal. These Sylves safeguard our desires and see that they are satisfied or transmuted to higher level from life to life and beyond. Even if you have evil desires, they must be catered to and satisfied- or transmuted for the good of the soul.

These water elementals– Sylves make it their home in the human psyche and our astral planes. We meet up with these Sylves in our in-between lives in the astrals to remind us of what we need to become. The Sylves change to each planetary system we incarnate to. Our soul's psyche houses them all no matter where we incarnate to. Our psyche is a vast place and quite universal. However, the rule is: each planetary system, multiverse, and Dimension has its own unique desires. You might wonder if there is a common thread that they all share?

Well, the common thread is revelations which foster wisdom. Revelation bridges the gap between all planetary systems, multiverses, and Dimensions in a way that is so personal- it is hard for me to put it into words- it changes per soul. Such wisdom is meant to be applied to have a universal awareness. Never mind all those travels with countless incarnations to magical realms – we can just do it all here upon the earth in due time just by being human!

Desires are all based on self-love, but they can be selfish desires that may hurt others too. We have been under many false concepts of selflessness in the age of Pisces, to the detriment of many people's better way of living. A false humility has caused them to live under their means by asking

153

very little from life. Being bound to the land like a serf in servitude to a lord has been abolished.

The era of the French Revolution (1790s to 1820s) saw serfdom abolished in most of Western and Central Europe, while its practice remained common in Eastern Europe until the middle of the 19th century (1861 in Russia). In France, serfdom had been in decline for at least three centuries before the start of the French Revolution, replaced by various forms of freehold tenancy.

The last vestiges of serfdom in France were officially ended on August 4, 1789, with a decree abolishing the feudal rights of the nobility. It removed the authority of the manorial courts, eliminated tithes and manorial dues, and freed those who remained bound to the land. However, the decree was mostly symbolic, as widespread peasant revolts had effectively ended the feudal system beforehand; and ownership of the land remained in the hands of the landlords, who could continue

154

collecting rents and enforcing tenant contracts. All of this had worked itself out in time as the modern age beckons. The industrial revolution did help to create a stronger middle-class system in Europe and in the present times.

We have long passed the age of Pisces with its servitudes and false humanities, combined with adherence to church authority. We are living in the era of free thinking and personal prosperity. Anyone with a desire can get some education and be rich in time. No longer are the nobles rich and serfs poor. We are living in the time of unbridled desires and prosperity. Yes, I will say this again – desires have lives of their own, and many Sylves live in us all and want our desires to be materialized.

In the age of Pisces, we as a human race were not awakened to have personal ego joys of our own. We should be glad to be alive in our present day where humanity and understandings of the disadvantages are felt and provided for. Living your

155

personal joy is very important to us in our age of enlightenment. We have been enlightening to the potential of man. I do not mean only a chosen few but everyone! I mentioned Ego joys for a reason. In the age of Pisces, only the nobility has Ego joys – not the common man. The common man was meant to serve their lords exclusively and forgo the little personal Ego joys of their own. Back then, one only had three choices – farming, crafts, or merchant marine work. I say little, but at least they had those choices back then.

Feeling like every day is Christmas with many presents is this Tattva made manifest and having all your desires come true. Now, we have all sorts of sweets to choose from, which is Apas – sweets. We have chocolates and all sorts of candies ready for us at stores. In the past, only food harvested in season was available to us – now we have access to them all year round. We are truly living in finer times now — the Apas Apas or watery part of water can fully be made manifest.

You might be asking yourselves: why were people so selfless in the past? The reason for this is that Europeans were to develop their character apart from human desires. Before the age of Pisces, governments and human relationships were barbaric. In the age of Pisces with the church as a stabilizing force created a lot of peace on the continent and fostered the love of virtues and fine character. Now, we want even more to be in the age of Aquarius.

If you should do magic or meditate on this Tattva, you could unearth many hidden desires that you previously thought you didn't have. You would also be awakened to your hidden psyche unknown to you before. You can start out being a housewife and with this magic, your dreams of becoming an actress or an artist could be awakened in time. There was a personality test I did in my youth from the

157

engram's neuropsychology studies that can reveal one hidden desire. I would not overlook that study!

What is Neuropsychology?

Neuropsychology is the study of brain-behavior relationships. A neuropsychological assessment is conducted to determine an individual's cognitive strengths and weaknesses. Moreover, Neuropsychology is a branch of psychology concerned with how a person's cognition and behavior are related to the brain, and the rest of the nervous system. Professionals in this branch of psychology often focus on how injuries or illnesses of the brain affect cognitive and behavioral functions.

George Ivanovic Gurdjieff brought a serving tray back from Afghanistan with a mysterious nine-point star on it. Gurdjieff taught that most humans do not possess the unified consciousness of themselves; and thus live their lives in a state of hypnotic "waking sleep". Furthermore, Gurdjieff states that it is possible to awaken these desires to a higher state of self-consciousness and achieve one's full human potential. He was told the story of this nine-pointed star with the nine-character types involved. George Ivanovic Gurdjieff used the story of the nine-character types with their interactions to understand the human psyche. To my research, this study had its origins in the delta of Egypt with the worship of the Ennead - The nine main Egyptian deities– Atum, Shu, Tephnut, Ged, Nut, Set, Asar, Nebt- het, and Aset. Outside of this arrangement are the Gods Heru, Subek, Serket, Tahuti, Het-heru and Ra.

You can even do past life repressions using this unique form of magic. I know many of my past lives, and had my last one as a Nazi guard who got depressed from being in a death camp and later turned into a Jesus freak who preached about Jesus to all who would care to listen. I was released from

159

the death camp to attend a university. In time, I was shot and died when the aliases forces were advancing into my university city that I was defending. I even had a parallel life roughly at the same time as my current life, but a little earlier. I was an American soldier serving in Vietnam who died as a lost captive just when the war was ending.

Between the two, and whatever type of psychoanalytic you feel comfortable with, it just might awaken your hidden psyche with all of its new desired formerly unknown to you.

To do these magic/ mediations, arrange the altar like the earlier one with a night blue cloth and draw a white crescent moon on the glass. Use rose or jasmine stick incense with some cold water and salt. Chant *Apas Apas* four times twice a day until the blue candle in glass burns down. The results will be a new you that had been previously unknown with a new psyche and a new destiny to be had.

160

This magic will make you very psychic and empathic as well. You would be able to read others' feelings and intent towards you. You could even use this magic to project positive vibes to others to heal bad relationships. This magic will open your heart to a greater love toward others who you have overlooked; and maybe nudge you to give them a phone call to say hello, and show that you do care.

Apas Agni or the
Fiery part of Water

The fiery part of water symbolizes a night blue field and a white crescent moon with an upward red triangle in its center. In nature, it is seen as fuel or in oil, alcohol, and gasoline. Alcohol was one of mankind's first joys. In the West, grapes and honey were made into wine. In Egypt, barley was fermented in beer. Later European made their own beer from this recipe with the addition of malts. In the east, rice was fermented into sake wine. These were mankind's first joys, along with honey as a food sweetener. There are some more types of fuel to mention: wood, candle wax, and coal. All of them are the earthly part of fire, though. Interestingly, Agni Prithvi is like a magnifying glass to the sun to start a fire.

The invention of gasoline took place nearly 160 years ago, as a byproduct of refining crude oil to make kerosene for lighters. No gasoline was used then, so it was burned at the refinery, converted to gaseous fuel for gas lights, or discarded. The term "gasoline" was first used in North America in 1864. In most Commonwealth countries (except Canada), the product is called "petrol" rather than "gasoline." The word petroleum, originally used to refer to various types of mineral oils and literally meaning "rock oil," comes from the medieval Latin word petroleum (Petra, "rock," and oleum, "oil").

Henry Ford and William Durant, along with bicycle mechanics J. Frank and Charles Duryea of Springfield, Massachusetts, had designed the first successful American gasoline automobile in 1893. They then won the first American car race in 1895, and went on to make the first sale of an American-made gasoline car the very next year.

First developed in France in the 1940s, the gas turbine has been utilized in many parts of the world. However, its service was short-lived. In North America, ALCO and GE developed various

163

gas-turbine locomotives for Union Pacific to power their various transcontinental trains; unfortunately, they were far less fuel-efficient than diesel. Nowadays, diesel is the fuel used in high-powered locomotives. One day, trains will all be electrically powered along with our long-awaited future automobiles.

Due to the invention of fuels such as refined oils, jet fuels, kerosene, and various types of gasoline, we can fuel the modern age of man today. One of the first fuels ever was ash. Ash was used to fuel iron refineries and to make steel. Most of England's forests were cut down to produce ash from burned wood. Many of England's Boggs were drained to make new farming land.

England had a mysteriously magical large forest before the industrial revolution came. I took a train ride north from London to Scottland and all I saw was flat grasslands with no trees at all; which previously had been a mystical forest with Boggs and odd stone formations like temples. Like coal, this ash is another element to cover – in the earthly part of the fire.

The heating of water to make steam was one of the first means of compulsion engines. Our early trains were fueled with coal to make steam to run them in the early days of transportation. The train systems opened the American West for settlers to start new communities and cities.

Anger is the fiery part of water as our emotions seem to boil with hot feelings of attacking others when threatened. Many men and lesbians seem to feel their anger more than other types. Here in New Orleans, la, people seem to feel their anger more than in other cities in the USA for some unknown reason. This land under the city of New Orleans was first used as an angry trading post for hundreds of years to establish these angry energies.

What does this mean to mankind apart from fuel and drinks? I can state two examples of the warm waters of the Caribbean and Florida. I even recall that in New Jersey; the ocean was quite warm in the summer months for swimming. Yes, there are many other places where the waters are delicate enough for swimming. We enjoy our hot baths, Jacques, steam rooms, and hot showers. Overall, the fiery part of the water is for comfort and convenience sacks. This Tattva adds luxury to our life and raises our standard of living. Without this Tattva, we wouldn't have our modern age as we know it now.

In the past, before the industrial revolution, the only means of expressing this element was in the preparation of food and hot Roman baths. This element was only recently awakened to its fullest. What we call electricity is the *fiery part of Aether*. We will cover that and the *earthy part of Fire* in due time in my writings.

166

On an emotional level, our emotions can be warmed to the boiling point with a new love relationship, a new job, new friends, a warming feel, a good film, a stage drama, an Opera production, a phone call from a special someone, a song well sung, a piece on your piano well played out, a pet who approached you to give you love, a child's smile, a job well done or just from reading a heart-warming book.

The Agni – fire element is akin to the Aether element of Akasha so spiritual bliss can be felt with this Tattva as well. Now, the Apas Akasha is very different but somewhat simpler. The way it is different is that in Apas of Akasha, we are dealing with mystical feelings that are foreign it us. We need those feelings to empower our souls here on Earth and elsewhere. I will write about that Tattva in due time in my work here. The Apas Agni deals with physical joys and splendors that are earthly and not spiritual. They may seem spiritual but in the light of Akasha, not really, as they are tangible feelings. The Apas Akasha deals with intangible feelings alone.

As you can see, this is a very important Tattva. To perform this magic/meditation, you need a night blue cloth with a blue candle in the glass. Draw a white crescent moon with an upward red triangle in its center. Chant *Apas Agni* four times twice a day until the candle burns down. You may use Acacia incense with the salt and water offerings as well.

Perform this type of magic/meditation if you are feeling sad and need your heart to be warmed. Do this practice to get you in a creative mood to draw or paint. Creative moods are significant here, being that Agni is creativity itself, and touching the emotional waters of life could create the mix of opposites that will combust into productivity and major accomplishments of an earthly value. If it were Apas of Akasha, it would have a heavenly

168

Aetheric value like spiritual clairvoyant visions of the future or visions of kingdoms unknown to mankind currently. Many Hindu sages had such experiences and wrote the Upanishads sad the Rig Vedas thousands of years ago in India.

This Tattva is one to pay attention to in your magical and meditative practices. It is one of my favorites among all of them. Have a copy of the symbol on your wall in your favorite room to remember this Tattva's energies and its chant –Apas Agni. Now, to better have these energies of this Tattva, it is best to share them with others. So, pick up the phone and share your love with a friend you know who is sad and needs encouragement. Give that special one a rose or bottle of men's cologne to show your love to him today.

This Tattva magic warms your emotional waters to the spiritual side of life. Your world will open to all humanity and pray for peace. The flame of Jesus Christ's love will warm you emotionally,

169

let you know that you are loved by God, and encourage you to love others. I like to think about Jesus with the flame in his heart or Yama ban with the divine couple in his heart. If this magic is done right, your heart will open to all sorts of loving expressions unknown to you.

Apas Vayu or the
Airy part of Water

A night blue field symbolizes the aetheric part of Water with a white crescent moon and a black teardrop egg in the center. The closest symbol in life might be a get-well card to a sick friend or family member. Your sympathetic feeling for others is a direct witness to this Tattva. Being considerate of other people's feelings is depicted here as well.

We all have human psyches and can feel for others as we think for ourselves. When we cannot, our characters experience a sense of deadness. If we continue to experience such deadness, it will lead to the death of the psyche. Once the psyche is dead, it needs to grow yet another psyche to replace it; this is undertaken to be had in the animal kingdoms, then to the human kingdom regrow a new psyche. The spirit is still alive as it always was and will be; however, its lower vehicle needs to be maintained

by respecting the most authentic nature of what it is
– love.

I will go into the understanding of what love really means. We have the three Gunas of Sattva, Tomas, and Raja, with the fourth Guna being A-Sattva, which is akin to Sattva but of a different nature. I will focus on Sattva and A-Sattva in this discussion now. Sattva is seen as good, sweet, kind, caring, and lovable. · A – Sattva has seen corrections given, discipline, and punishments.

Many people do not realize that the Holocaust was for a reason. Millions of souls were guilty of mass murder on a national level in wars who needed to get their karmic retributions over with. This retribution was the Holocaust; the good German people took the lead in its administration. Many disasters and misfortune happen to others for a good reason; this law is the law of reflections. We are the other person, and if you act selfishly and in hate, you will receive retribution in due time.

172

This law of reflection is what the Master Jesus spoke about in his Golden Rule. The fact remains the other person, and you are true to oneself and not two. Only one child of God is experienced in an infinite diffusion of souls. Our most authentic nature is that we are ONE! Feeling this oneness on an emotional and psyche level is the definition of the Tattva, the Aetheric part of Water or Apas Akasha.

In John 14:9, what is meant by the scripture, *"He who has seen me has seen the Father?"*

Jesus and his Father are one, but not how Jesus tries to tell you. They are one in heart, mind, purpose, and spirit. They are separate but working together in complete harmony and cooperation—Jesus in total subjection to his Father. Philip is asking Jesus to show them the Father, and Jesus is saying, "if you see me, you are also seeing the Father because we are in complete agreement; we have the same nature and the same spirit."

Philip asks how we can know the ways of heaven. We can be grateful that Philip asked this question because we have Jesus' answer on record. "I am the way, the truth, and the life; no man cometh unto the Father but by me." It was only possible to reach the Father by first accepting the Son. So, what does it mean to take the Son? What does assuming that we are all one under one sonship mean? Jesus used himself to represent the very fact that the sonship of God is infinite and uncountable in its numbers.

This Tattva can be experienced when you feel the pain and joy of others. The aetheric nature of Apas – Water comes out in this Tattva. The feeling of donating a dollar to a homeless man or woman is felt here; it is the feeling that you care for others. If you can open your heart to your own lovable psyche, you will feel the oneness amongst you all. You just might be giving to charities without any

174

reward or gala dinners, or certificates of donations made public in the new papers.

The feeling that you, and the other person feel this oneness, but at the same time, you are not taken advantage of. You just cannot let homeless people into your own homes and let them steal from you. It would help if you had your boundaries in place. When helping someone escape the mud, you do not let yourselves be pulled into it. Caring for the God within you is self-love. We must care for the inner God within ourselves too. We must maintain our sense of peace in our homes. If our children are screaming and acting up, remember to have patience with them. They will grow up, and it is best to appreciate how lovely they are at their age, regardless of how they act and scream.

Feeling empathic is another manifestation of this Tattva. When I started developing my psychic skills many years ago in New York City, I practiced Psychometry. I learned many psychic symbols to

175

read by; Psychometry involves holding another person's object and allowing psychic impression to register with you emotionally; this is an Empathic way of practicing. There is a clairvoyant way of doing the same: the Aetheric part of fire or Agni Akasha. It involves seeing images in your third eye like a television dropping down upon your frontal vision. We will cover that later in the book, but now we can discuss empathic connections with others.

My mother is very psychic. She seems to know what is going on in my life without me telling her. My mother's grandmother on her Father's side was blind but navigated throughout her house as if she had eyes like a bat. My mother got that same psychic gift from her, and I got it from my mother in a likewise manner. Remember that the psychic impressions here are through one's emotional channel and not the third eye, which is another Tattva altogether.

Empathy and compassion are both fruits of this Tattva. You can feel this oneness through your emotional channels; this is where the emotions are blessed by Lord Vishnu and ignited by Lord Krishna and Christ; this is where a physical no, divine element of made semi-divine to uplift us all and help us be liberated from the Maya of our own soul stuck in the material.

Again, the A -Satva needs to be understood, which is karma under the law of reflections. You are fooling yourself; you think that you can get away by being evil. All evil deeds are brought to justice in time. We had the Russian/Ukraine war because of Putin's feeling of vulnerability for the West. The truth is – man of God has no vulnerabilities at all. Putin acted like a mortal human, not a divine son of God. I prayed for the Ukrainian people and their victory! That was my Illuminati work for now, I felt. We might gain some insights into this by understanding two things below:

177

1.   A-Satva is discipline and punishments. We all need challenges for growth. There is a Chinese Hanzi for chaos, disorder, and evil - Wěn luàn, which is the same Hanzi meaning growth; this seems to entail that all world evil is needed for us as a challenge for us all to grow. A – Satva is also doing things you prefer not to do, but you do anyway for their benefits; you will see the results in time (for e.g. schoolwork, weightlifting, punishing children, imprisonment, etc).

2.   Tomas' immaturity leads to evil behavior. Such behavior will be met with the law of reflectivity and A – Satva in one learning to gain maturity.

One last thing to mention is the impression one gains from reading spiritually inspired books. In my lifetime, I have read many of them. One book created five psychological catharses to help me against the inner torments I was experiencing in my

178

youth – *A course in miracles*. I was tormented by an astrological transit that lasted around three years, but my self-help book on creating Miracles got me out of my torments back then. The book helped me to work directly with my psyche to alleviate my inner sufferings. I felt that I had a schizophrenic attack and was afraid to seek help for what I was experiencing. I felt that my astrology ignited this section as well, for me to share and clear through it; that reason for its clearing, I still do not know even to this day – the way of the psyche is mysterious to us, I believe. I am left to leave it as such.

You can even create such catharsis with a therapist or read a good psychological book on self-understanding. Just allow the correct mode to allow such catharsis to come to you. Catharsis is a psychological breakthrough of the subconscious mind to the conscious mind; this is genuinely the light shining in the dark! May your light forever shine!

179

To perform that Tattva magic/mediation, lay out an orange tablecloth with a blue candle in its center. With a blue marker draw a blue ball; then with black marker, draw a black teardrop egg in the center of that in the glass of the 7-day novella candle. Chant *Apas Akasha* four times twice a day until the candle burns out. You can also post an image of this Tattva. The magic will work like rubbing alcohol to cleanse areas of your life that are negative and in need of healing. You can even do this magic for others with addictions so they may be clean of the drugs in their bodies.

Agni- Fire

Agni Tattva, or a red upward triangle in a field of green

Agni– fire represents our very own Spirit manifesting in these realms of duality. The fire is unstable; however, it needs four other elements to stabilize it. Its symbol in nature is a flaming campfire in the cool night sky.

When we were first born into this odd realm of duality, only stars were in the night sky. Planets were not yet formed. The universe was very new, as well as life itself. We dwelled in the heart of stars, only to emerge once the planet was ready to support life. We then had to grow beyond these stars, so we entered the water element and lived in outer space and the numerous astral realms - Astral meaning heavenly. The Air and Earth Realms were created simultaneously; then, physical life on the planet was possible.

182

Life in the stars was quite heavenly and regal. We all acted through each other to be kings. Even though the king was without number, each king ruled as if they were the only one, and all obeyed him – however, each king held the same claim; this is just one mystery of the fire element. The same is true here in our realm of the Earth – we have, for the most part, forgotten this fact. If you can hand an unloved woman a rose, such an act might ignite a massive cloud of gas in the universe to create a new star. Who is to say that it will not?

Our consciousness exists between the fire and air elements. When we did not have the air element of the Mind, we used our inner sense of knowingness to rule the heavens. The air element truly is the small-mindedness of humanity. The Mind's nature is to think from its own perspective only– with the *I am*. All world philosophies attempt to understand this small-minded I in a universal

183

way. In some ways, it is true, but like the Air element, it is not valid.

In the fire element, we find the laws of the universe. We are bound to these laws anywhere we go: it may be the lofty astral realms or the physical world, we are still bound to these laws; we are made as one through the fire element as one flame of God in his hand. The dual nature of the odd realms we have chosen to experience has created uncountable multitudes of this one flame. According to the laws of God, if it does exist, it always has existed with no beginning or end. God allows every one of us to rule His living environments as if we are the only God ourselves. However, doing so will cause one to demonstrate this rule accurately for himself. So, one falls from his graces with God to be a God-made manifest.

Our current riddle of God is just one of many riddles of God to mention - an uncountable number of riddles that causes one to leave God's graces and

184

go to self-deluded realms like the one we are in currently.

The law of love is a fiery law; this law can stand as the only law one needs to adhere to. Love is a warm campfire on a freezing night. One can cook their food as we have done in our small communities over the last two million years. The fire element creates community. The campfire brings together a group of people who, in time, seem to know you better than you know yourself.

I recall my army day in Fort Polk, Louisiana. I remember that the platoon knew me in ways I did not know myself. I was a seeker of negative attention back then. The platoon seemed to see that army life was not for me, so I was discharged in a brief period. I later started to collect a disability package from the military that supports me with my social security. My army service proved essential to my thriving lifestyle over these nineteen years. I

185

believe in our USA army and am glad I tried to serve my country.

Let us now consider the graphic image of the fire – Agni element. The image is of a red upward triangle in a field of green. The area of green is the heart's chakra color and represents – Love. The upward triangle represents the divine Spirit of God inherited in all of God's sons. This Divine Spirit is singular but made into an uncountable infinite mass in these realms of duality. By the right hand of God, we are mysteriously at one with the sons of God, as a flame in God's hand, and the infinite and eternal diversity of God's sons; this is such a mystery that only God seems to understand how this phenomenon can happen.

Above the thirteen-Dimension, we are out of the fire element, and unconscious. Even though unconscious, it is awakened to a universal consciousness unknown to us here on the Earth. We are outside the four elements of Earth, Water, Fire,

186

and Air. We are in the Aetheric Realms of Aether: this is the fifth element, and its nature is like the Agni – fire element but beyond the one point – I ness of the ego self. This Fire element is semi-divine but caters to this one pointed – I ness of the ego. The passions of our human nature and fighting are of this fire element. There is a lower and higher manifestation of the fire- Agni element.

The lower manifestation of fire is anger and fighting, due to the air element's influence of small-mindedness that it has over the fire element. The key to not getting angry is to think things out more deeply and broadly. Many people who have bipolar mental illness are mad throughout the day and react with anger quite often to the minor things, to the larger of them both. Viewing life in the manner of how it affects us is small-minded thinking. There are reasons and motives behind people's actions and words, and to judge them at face value is not using a fire-inspired intellect.

187

When the fire element affects the air element of the Mind, we become innovative. The fire in the Mind brought humanity from primitive times to the modern times we live in now. The fire of Mind is the understanding of world mythology, higher math, metaphysics, philosophy, sociology, and psychology.

Our Earth's Mother did not want us to have this fire of Mind. In Greek mythology, Prometheus is one of the Titans, the supreme trickster, and a god of fire. In common belief, he developed into a master craftsman; and in this connection, he was associated with fire and the creation of mortals. Prometheus gave fire to humanity, and his punishment was to have his liver eaten out of his body every night by vultures.

This story shows that Gaia did not wish for humanity to have this fire of Mind; however, to live just slightly above the animal kingdom along with nature like the natives of ancient North America did before the Europeans took over and modernized them. The American Indians made our Earth Mother very happy; if it were up to her, we would all live on that level. If it were up to her, Gaia would open to her people the mysteries of our universe in mythology and stories about campfires.

However, mankind got its hands on the fire element and became innovative. Gaia, our Earth Mother, knew of the complications of the innovations of mankind and the dangers they may hold. Now, we are to work these issues out for ourselves. Gaia has come to terms with us as a race having this fire of Mind and will help us to progress to the stars and elevate our cities over the land. Gaia wishes for us to have very little influence over our earthly environment, and live at one with it.

The laws of the fire: Agni element is love, community, family, laughter, drama, athletics, joy, and celebrations. Yes, joy is a fruit of this fire element. It is essential to have a shared sense of this

189

joy. What I mean by shared is that all are made happy and have a part in this joy. It is, therefore, not a selfish joy but a universal joy. The fire element is personal and not universal as its parent is the aether element. The fire element Agni resembles universal joy but love on a personal level.

To perform the magic of Agni, we must lay out our green tablecloth with a red candle in glass. Draw on the glass the upward red triangle. Light acacia incense or cinnamon and chant the word *Agni* four times, twice a day until the candle burns out. Your heart will be open to a personal joy that only you can appreciate – it might resemble a universal pleasure, but in a unique way.

Agni Prithvi or the Earthly part of Fire

A green field symbolizes the earthly part of Fire with an upward red triangle and a yellow square in the center of the triangle. This Tattva is physical Fire. What it does, is that it creates physical Fire like a flame. We use Fire for cooking, and heating up our homes. Our physical Sun is of this element of the fiery part of Earth.

Our Sun is a fireball that combusts *hydrogen*. Our Sun, like most stars, during the main phase of its lifetime, creates energy by fusing hydrogen atoms in its core. In about 5 billion years, the Sun will start running out of hydrogen in its core to fuse and grow into a red giant.

Our Sun is 4,500,000,000 years old; this will make its total life span 9.5 billion years. Our universe is said to be 14 billion years old by now. Our Sun's arrival in the timeline makes it a late bloomer. Our solar system's previous Sun was much more massive and created many heavy elements that are still found in our solar system today. That Sun probably lived for just a few billion years. One day the surface of our Sun will grow, evaporate our ocean, and melt our planet's surface. By then, Mercury and Venus would have been swallowed by our Sun, and our planet would be the next to go! By then, who knows what humanity could have evolved into or where we might be. I heard of a radio broadcast for help from a dying planet in the past. Who is to say if it is a true story, but why bother lying about it? Let us say it is true that the planet did die – it could happen to us one day!

Firewood, fire, and coal are three physical representations of this Tattva in nature. Our early train system used coal to fire its engine to create steam to run the pistons to create motion. In the past, we mainly used firewood to prepare food and warm our baths. Only recently have we begun to use alternative means of creating heat, or fire.

In our human psyches, this Tattva manifests as a physical vision of the eyes or, to put in other words - our perceptions of others and life. I once read a book called – *A Course in Miracle*, which teaches that *a miracle is a change in perception. If we can change how we look at the world, the world will change.*

What does change is how the world reflects on us. Love will reflect on us in time if we see a precious planet. This book, *A Course in Miracle,* is a plagiary of Christian Science religion taught by Mary Baker Eddy, *not Scientology,* with Tom Cruise and John Travolta. The lessons in the back of the book are based on Zen observations; This makes this book *A Course in Miracles,* a new age phenomenon self-help book.

Changing one's perceptions is the basis of all psychoanalytical workings. If I can do it with a self-help book – *A Course in Miracles*, so can you with any psychological book that attracts you. I mentioned this book in the Akasha Apas chapter; however, the aetheric Element resembles the Agni element of Fire here.

The concept of working itself is akin to this Tattva, the earthly part of Fire. We all need to work to maintain our communities, nation, and the world that we are a part of. I have been retired for nineteen years now. I used to work for an airline and then as a waiter for parties. In my retirement, I am trying to work as a profitable new age, quantum, and occult writer.

I tried to create jewelry as a computer aid design operator, but I was seen as not suitable for the office, though I did qualify. I make many jewelry pieces for myself; I outdid my jewelry school days with the most contemporary jewelry I

194

created in CAD. I am also working on a music composition book for the harp. Music compositions are challenging, and a high amount of skill is required.

I find it impossible not to be working at any age. Work is an essential part of living. In this world, most industrial peoples and nations have higher living standards and a better quality of living. Finland, Canada, and Denmark, respectively, have the highest standard of living in the world.

This is not to say that the wealthiest nation, the United States of America, has a problem with its standard of living. The three I mentioned have well-balanced and suitable social and medical systems to serve people. Being socialist, though, who knows when you will have treatments in the hospital for emergency operations? In the USA, you can get it fast as long as you pay for it. Our disadvantaged middle class finds it hard to get medical insurance if not through the companies they work for.

195

The sparks from Agni fires are akin to this Tattva. Forest fires ignite due to foot traffic in such arid forests. We have used sparks to create our Fire for millions of years now. Our stove and oven still use sparks to ignite the gas flames.

A nuclear warhead has an ignition built inside, as nuclear power plants do. Sparking an ignition is this Tattva; meaning is akin to the ability to *work*. As a result of the spark of nuclear fusion, we now have low-cost electrical power. How is atomic energy sparked up in power plants? Well, I will explain now.

A nuclear reactor produces and controls the release of energy from splitting the atoms of Uranium. In a nuclear power reactor, the energy released is used as heat to make steam that in turn, generates electricity.

The principles for using nuclear power to produce electricity are the same for most reactors.

The energy released from continuous fission of the atoms of the fuel is harnessed as heat in either a gas or in water, and then is used to produce steam. Steam is used to drive the turbines which produce electricity (as in most fossil fuel plants).

The world's first nuclear ore deposit of Uranium developed in nature about two billion years ago. These were in rich uranium ore bodies and moderated by percolating rainwater. The 17 known at Oklo in West Africa, each less than 100 kW thermal, consumed about six tons of Uranium together.

We can assume that these pressurized water reactors (PWR) have water at over 300°C under pressure in their primary cooling/heat transfer circuit and generate steam in a secondary circuit. The less numerous boiling water reactors (BWR) make steam in the primary circuit above the reactor core at similar temperatures and pressure. Both types use water as both coolant and moderator to

197

slow neutrons. Since water boils typically at 100°C, they have robust steel pressure vessels or tubes for higher operating temperatures. Other types of uses were not unique worldwide.

Today, reactors derive from designs developed initially for propelling submarines and large naval ships that generate about 85% of the world's nuclear electricity. The main structure is heavy water, with deuterium atoms as moderators. Hence the term 'light water' is used to differentiate it from the older versions.

Art is accredited to this Tattva. Being that art is a work of vision – vision being of the fire element and the materialization of your vision is of the earthly – Prithvi element. Art has been a part of our world's culture since the origin of humanity. What I mean by art is not just European paintings but world art. We have oriental vases with ink painting on silk. We also have sculptures in marble and bronze from our ancient European past. We have

198

Native American jewelry as well. In our modern age, we now have digital art and cartooning for children's pleasure.

The French artists Georges Seurat and Paul Signac invented pointillist art- the revolutionary painting technique that (eventually became known as *Pointillism)* attempted to use the *science of optics* when creating paintings; this was made by painting small but separate dots of unmixed colors side by side, which were placed in various patterns to form an image.

This effect was that placing the dots so close to one another would automatically blur an image into the viewers' eyes. This technique resembles how computer screens work today, as the pixels correspond to the dots in a Pointillism painting. In a vision, George Seurat saw television and computer screens' uses back in the 1880s – 1890s.

199

Pointillism art reinvented the use of painting with small dabs of paint made famous by the Impressionist movement to the point where artists attempted to produce an entire artwork out of these little dots of pure color. Therefore, it is considered part of the post-Impressionist movement. It rose in popularity between the 1880s and 1890s after the Impressionist period had ended.

One may wonder why artists went through so much trouble developing this innovative yet uniquely complex technique; this was simply because they wanted to remodel and transform what art school was teaching them. In doing so, they could present a new definition of what it meant to be an artist.

Architecture is a form of art on a grand scale. Ancient Greek and Roman buildings are still seen today as quite classic in their designs. Gothic and Romanesque churches are appreciated today as they were in their origins a century ago. If I had a wish, the cathedral of Saint John the Divine could be finished in 20 years if it could arrange its financing. This church gave ever so much for the World War II effort, they forgot themselves.

Who cares about rewarding bankrupt churches nowadays? La Sagrada Familia of Barcelona, Spain is almost fully constructed now; this is an undertaking that took hundreds of years, so why can't we finance the remaining constructions of St John the Divine? I read Saint John the Divine can't be built as designed. They have a water table under the cathedral, which isn't good for such a heavy structure.

The human Ego is another manifestation of this Tattva. The Fire of Agni can be made stable in one's identification of themselves. We all have things that we identify with, like a name, country, gender, age, etc. These are the building blocks of a healthy psyche. Can you see now how the fire and

201

water elements are akin to each other – they co-exist with each other; they cannot ever be set apart?

The human Ego protects us from harm, and its home is our skin; it sees other egos as friends or foes. The human Ego is dramatic; it works out its drama in relationships, work, and social groups. This Tattva wants to answer the riddle of who God is by being a god; this is the very definition of egotism – the godman made manifest. We seem to use this warped expression of trying to understand God better, but we never seem to reach that level.

Creativity is another manifestation of the Tattva. I enjoy life drawings of the nude body. One day, I will learn watercolor. Artwork is such a relaxing practice; it works on the focus of your vision into the material – the earthly part of Fire. I should try to attend my life drawing sessions more often. My work as a pencil and paper artist is developing nicely- I must keep up with it. I also enjoyed in my lifetime, terracotta clay sculpting

202

of mythological deities. I put them on my altar as a sign of devotion to the deity. Yes, I do enjoy Wicca! I like Egyptian Wicca in particular.

We can see that this Tattva has a diverse meaning, all teh way from the ability to do work, perceptions, egotism, and creativity; to a campfire, art, and nuclear energy. All in all, the earthly part of Fire is essential to life on Earth.

How can you perform magic / meditate with this Tattva? You might need its energy to clean your house and yard or do artwork, or you might need to change how you perceive a situation or a person for the better.

If that is the case, prepare green clothes as a table covered with a red candle in glass. Draw an upward red triangle on the glass with a red marker and a yellow square in the center of that triangle. Chant the words *Agni Prithvi* four times twice a day until the candle burns out. You may use the symbol of this Tattva as a visual aid to remember its energies. With this magic, you can ignite the drama of life itself. Go out and be the star that you are!

Agni Apas or the
Watery part of Fire

The watery part of Fire symbol is a field of green with an upward red triangle in its center with a crescent moon in the center of that triangle. The two elements are opposite, with fire being a positively charged element and water being a negatively charged element. The result is the combustion of force – the essence of energy itself – the Lord Krishna. This Tattva is also speed, velocity, movements, and travel. This element gives life to all other elements. In this element, fire acts as if it were water. How can this be in nature? A forest fire can be pretty fluid as it burns a massive forest area. Fire does have a fluid manner to its nature in the way that it can spread itself widely.

We need forest fires to renew the forest from time to time. Some pinecones are only open with the heat of a forest fire. These "serotinous" cones can hang on a pine tree for years, long after the enclosed seeds mature. Only when a fire sweeps through, melting the resin, do these heat-dependent pinecones open - releasing seeds that are then distributed by wind and gravity. As you can see, nature has prepared itself for such forest fires.

The use of magic is under this Tattva. I hope you will be practicing in a magical way using these Tattva. Witchcraft is primarily of the fire Agni element; however, with the use of the human psyche to fulfill his desires, the water element of Apas comes into play. Indeed, magic is of the akashic level; when it is common play with humanity, it becomes – fire – Agni.

We continue to the water element of Apas to appease as our desires. Magic has a very long history on our planet. In the times of antiquities, humanity has been engaged with magic. In the past, we did not have the technology we do today to assist us in life; we had to use magic to meet our daily needs.

206

I say again, I am a practitioner of Egyptian magic with some traditional Wicca added to my practice. My magic in New Orleans is stronger here than in other cities. New Orleans is a city of many characters like magic, jazz- Jazz fest with Jazz on Frenchman st, parades- Mardi Gras, and charity gala balls. It is also an affordable southern city with warm winters and entertainment. That is why I live here currently. In time, I will move back to South Florida to be by the clear blue ocean and the city's nightlife.

One underlying commonality amongst all the definitions of this Tattva is – action! The (spark of the earthly part of fire) ignites the (gas vapors – the fiery part of water) in the cylinders of your car to create a movement of its wheels – (travel! – The watery part of fire!) As you can see from my writings, these Tattva do work together.

Velocity is yet one more aspect of this Tattva. A jet running down the runway reaches a certain speed then, with the help of its wings, it takes to the sky. The air's current is what maintains the jet traveling through the sky. We have flight between the forward thrust of the jet engines and the wing design. Velocity is the result of this. Commercial aircraft typically fly at around 460-575 mph or 740-930 km/h. between its velocity and wig design, we have air travel; this is one of the modern conveniences we have today.

They say that in the future, we will be traveling in the outer parts of our atmosphere near outer space and reach unheard-of speeds. Air travel will be far less time-consuming than it is currently. The flight from New York City to Tokyo, Japan, might be only two hours. This mode of travel might only be good for long distances and not short runs like New Orleans to Houston, Texas.

When our great spirit sees that we need a change in our lives, it speaks to us through this element of the watery part of fire. These powerful

208

words of our spirit speak as if it were God Himself. These comments are silent, but their effects will be made apparent through the individual by means of a personal revelation. This fire of Mind stirs the inner nature of our psyche, making us realize a new way of thinking and being.

Our psyches make themselves warm in the fire element of Agni. We feel spiritual and at one with our God. Our psyches – the water element - God's inner presence- enlighten Apas. Between the two, the mysteries of God surfaced through the steam created by this Tattva – Agni Apas. I said earlier that this is an essential Tattva. Now, you are starting to realize that for yourselves. The color of this Tattva should be a passionate purple. You may substitute a purple candle with a traditional red one instead if it makes you feel better.

Clairvoyant visions are akin to this Tattva. Many spiritual people had something very close to a direct witness with God using clairvoyance. I

209

personally had many clairvoyant visions in my lifetime; they come in in our greatest hours of need. The magic of it is how it moves up to the right actions for benefit our lives.

Explosions are akin to this Tattva. We use dynamite to explode rocks and tree stumps and for the fireworks to celebrate the holiday. Dynamite, a blasting explosive patented in 1867 by the Swedish physicist Alfred Nobel. Dynamite is based on nitroglycerin but is much safer to manage than nitroglycerin alone. By mixing nitroglycerin with kieselguhr - a porous siliceous Earth, in proportions that left a dry and granular material. Nobel produced a solid that was resistant to shock but readily detonable by heat or percussion. Later, wood pulp in the explosive substituted as an absorbent agent. After that, sodium nitrate was added as an oxidizing agent to increase the strength of the explosive as a ncw development.

Forgiveness is akin to this Tattva of the watery part of fire. What is truly meant by the word forgiveness is that the offense is no longer affecting your psyche – it has been burned away. We think that we have forgiven someone, but if the injury still influences you psychologically, you have not followed through with the process.

Romantic relationships have always been impossible for me. All I had was two lovers in my life, but many affairs and good friends with one bad friend who damaged my psyche in a short time. These bad associations may create injuries that submerge from our subconscious minds for healing in time, or manifest as these associations for us to heal them or learn a lesson.

I recently had an issue involving my army days, but it has passed now. One of the keys to understanding incarnation better is why we need to relive them. The reason to relive these old injuries is to heal them and get them out of our subconscious

211

minds. There are times when we cannot forgive. We need to hold on to these bad memories to protect ourselves. There are parental issues that I have not forgiven yet, but then again, I was a difficult child to handle.

In the inward journey of self-understanding, we have this Tattva's influences. We gain knowledge with the fiery part of air —Vayu Agni, however, with no knowledge required to achieve an inner experience – only an inner sense of freedom is needed. I can understand this as the silent journey of the soul. No words can even come close to expressing the experiences one has on this inner journey.

The American Indians sent their youth on a vision quest in the wilderness to find them. Jesus Christ wandered in the desert for forty days and was tempted by his inner devil to be selfish and not serve humanity. He did not listen to his inner devil but ignored it; he when on to be a world savior in time.

212

If one tried to put words to this silent journey, one would be fooling themselves as words cannot justify the unmentioned experiences of this journey.

What a Vision quest is, is a supernatural experience in which an individual seeks to interact with a guardian spirit, usually an anthropomorphized animal, to obtain advice or protection. Vision quests were most typically found amongst the native peoples of North and South America.

The specific techniques for attaining visions varied from tribe to tribe, as did the age at which the first Quest was to be undertaken, its length and intensity, and the expected form of the guardian spirit's presence or sign. In some tribes, nearly all young people traditionally engaged in some vision quest. Their participation in the experience was an ancient ritual marking an individual's transition from childhood to adulthood. In other native cultures, vision questing was undertaken only by

213

males, with menarche and childbirth as analogous experiences for females. Some groups, notably in South America, limited vision quests and guardian spirits to shamans (this is a religious personage with powers of healing and psychic transformation).

Usually, an individual's first vision quest was preceded by a period of preparation with a religious specialist. The Quest typically involved going to an isolated location and engaging in prayer while forgoing food and drink for up to several days; some cultures augmented fasting and prayer with hallucinogens. In some traditions, the participant would watch for an animal that behaved in a significant or unusual way; in others, the participant discovered an object (often a stone) that resembled some animal. In the predominant form, the initiate had a dream (the vision) in which a spirit appeared.

Upon receiving a sign or vision, the participant returned home and sought help interpreting the experience. Not all vision quests

214

were successful; religious specialists generally advised individuals to abandon a given attempt if a vision was not received within a prescribed time.

The advice and protection are a superficial reward of this Quest. The real rewards are maturity and taking responsibility for oneself as an adult. I would not go on a Vision Quest to obtain knowledge and protection, as both are worthless. The real reward is inner growth and a sense of divinity gained. This divinity cares throughout one's life and protects one from danger and mistreatment from others. If one has a good understanding of their inner divinity, they will act appropriately, not foolishly or rudely.

Above all, the Tattva of the watery part of fire – Agni Apas is one of the essential Tattva to perform magic. We need influence in our lives to inspire us to a higher way of living. If you can, try to chant the Agni Apas throughout the day for inner strength and maturity to handle the significant issues in life.

Now, to perform magic/mediation with this Tattva, set out your green tablecloth with your red or purple candle in glass. Draw red upward triangle with the crescent moon in silver in its center, and chant *Agni Apas* four times twice a day. If your magic is done right, God's voice could be heard by you and direct you to your highest levels of life experiences.

Agni Agni, or the Fiery part of Fire

The fiery part of the fire symbol is a green field with a red upward triangle in its center, with yet another red upward triangle in the center of that triangle. Its symbol in nature is vision. We can only represent vision by using human eyes.

Vision first evolved about 530 million years ago during the Cambrian explosion, but they were jawless and without eyes – only sensors pad wired to their brains. The first fish arose in the Ordovician Period (about 485 million to 444 million years ago) and radiated extensively in the Devonian Period (about 419 million to 359 million years ago).

Fish fossils from these periods have eye sockets, indicating that these fish must have had eyes. Vision, as we know it is dated between 419 to 359 million years old ago. The first eyes were flat pads, but over time they became deeper until a spherical shape evolved. The eyes evolved inward in the heads of the Cambrian-era fish for their protection; this became a norm for all future fish and carried on when fish walked the land to evolve into the first dinosaurs. From that point, the evolution continued to the era of mammals, then apes, then to man.

The first eyes were just a plate of nerves connected to the flatworm's early brains, which were relatively small. This *flatworm*, also called *platyhelminth*, is a crucial step in the evolution of life on our planet. As fish evolved, so did its eyes. This early flatworm consciously gained the advantage of navigation.

Before the evolution of eyes, early fish life in the Cambrian Ocean was subconscious, like today's jellyfish. The development of vision and consciousness goes hand in hand. To see – or have vision – is to know! Therefore, we have consciousness. So, I might claim that the fiery part of Fire also represents consciousness. Most possibly, it does, to my research; however, the air element - brain must also be present. I can safely say that the flatfish was the first fish with a conscious mind. The flatfish could decide amongst many possibilities given for its well-being and survival.

When did humanity become fully conscious? You may wonder if society is fully aware of our current problems. We eat meat from the animals we bully; we eat fish from the ocean on a grand level; we pollute our lands and waters; we have senseless wars with no end.

They say that both the Buddha and Christ were awakened individuals. Their ways were of peace and goodwill to others. They both left worldly values to take up, which are beyond our minds' scope. Humanity is still in its animal body and not fully awakened. Have you wondered why our brothers from various planets in outer space are not

219

amongst us now? The answer is that we are not evolved enough to relate to them on their level.

Consciousness began when animals such as birds and mammals developed much larger brains with hundreds of millions of neurons, around 200 million years ago. Consciousness began with humans - Homo sapiens, approximately 200,000 years ago. Please, keep in Mind that I said – began! So, what am I referring to by the word – Consciousness? Well, as far as I can tell, humanity will reach a level of consciousness greater than many leagues of angels and most of our alien outer space brothers someday.

So, what is meant by the word Consciousness? *con·scious·ness*

- The quality or state of being aware, especially of something within oneself.

- The state or fact of being conscious of an external object, state, or fact.

- AWARENESS is especially concerned for some social or political causes.

- The organization aims to raise the political consciousness of teenagers.

- The state of being characterized by sensation, emotion, volition, and thought MIND.

- The totality of conscious states of an individual.

- The normal state of conscious life regained *consciousness*. The upper level of the mental life of which the person is aware is contrasted with unconscious processes.

I have heard the phrase in the New Age community – **to raise one's consciousness.** So, what does it mean to raise one's consciousness? From what I know, it means to think on a broader and more vast level. That level involves considering

221

all living creatures' rights to life and living with mankind. If we could do this much, we would be on a much higher level of life. So, why don't we make the adjustments now? The answer is – our sense of worthlessness. We do not have higher self-esteem to ask for better than what we currently have. I feel that self-love and self-worth will take us to a new future beyond the scope of Mind we now possess— all it will take from us is a little self-love and self-worth.

The fiery part of Fire can also be seen as God's greatest unknowable. This unknown leaves us with another thing for our self-help – personal revelations. We need these revelations to loosen up the restrictive hold that our earth element may have upon us all. Yes, the Earth is good for us, but it can also be limiting. The God vibration is 144,000 Hz, and the Earth and universe are much lower – remember that!

The fiery part of Fire can also be called the motivation that moves us to do things. So, from where do we get such motivation? The answer is from our spirits! Have you ever just done something without even thinking about it beforehand? This behavior is called compulsory action. We will discuss the required action and mandatory action now.

The main difference between mandatory and compulsory lies in their usage. Mandatory indicates a quality of binding to the thing, while compulsory suggests a necessity of something. Both mandatory and compulsory are two words that mean something essentially different. Therefore, these two words are often used as synonyms. Nevertheless, they have different meanings concerning their usage.

What I am referring to here is compulsory, which is the necessity of doing something right for you at that given moment. The fiery part of the Fire is the feeling of doing what is right on a compulsory

223

level. When I was a child, I was told not to hit girls. Is this a tradition, or is it the right course of action?

Well, hitting anyone is wrong, even children. There are just better ways of correcting than hitting. Knowing the right course of action, you must first not be mad and reactionary to situations. You must be in control of yourself. Never allow yourself to be ruled by your anger. Anger is an immature reaction to protect your vulnerabilities. If you are strong in who you are, you will not have any vulnerabilities. Child abuse passes itself down from one generation to the next. Some parents are self-confident enough to have a finer way to correct their children than abusing them.

Doing what is right in the world takes group cooperation. The United States of America, the European Union, and the United Nations are working for world peace. Our world's moral standards condone wars. Most of the world supports Ukraine's people's right to sovereignty as a nation and not as a puppet nation of the Russian Federation. Donating to the groups defending human rights in Ukraine might be an excellent time.

We are doing what is proper means – action and not just sitting on your sofa and thinking about it- but doing it! We could donate to the Red Cross to support the Ukrainian people. However, the developed world is just as guilty for polluting our planet with greenhouse gases and raising the world temperature by a few degrees. Will our coastal cities have to be flooded for us to come to our senses? When will you consider alternative foods besides animal products? The divine flame of the fiery part of Fire, or Agni Agni, is not shining bright enough in our world to transform us to a new level. Once we are on that all-new level, our outer space neighbors will join us in a unique celebration of the Earth.

Does this fiery part of Fire have a dangerous side to it? Yes, it is anger! Now, here are ways to

225

control and understand our rage. Let us consider just a few of them now!

Anger is often closely tied to addiction. It is a normal response to the hurt caused by trauma, abuse, or neglect. However, many people do not deal with their anger healthily. They lose control and become aggressive or violent, or they repress their anger, leading to depression and anxiety.

People habitually stop anger, often because they learn early on that their anger will be punished and may become the passive-aggressive type; or they may resort to sarcasm, stonewalling, or avoidance when someone makes them angry, instead of addressing the problem.

Whether prone to violent outbursts or passive aggression, the unskillful expression of anger can alienate those who care about you. Having supportive friends and family is essential for everyone and is crucial for recovering from addiction. If anger is a problem for you, here are some more constructive ways to express it.

Pause: The first and most important thing to do is notice when you're getting angry and don't make any decisions while in the grip of anger. When you're mad, your judgment, foresight, and self-control are non-existent, so anything you do impulsively out of anger will most likely worsen things. Take some deep breaths and calm down, then decide what you want to do.

Identify your emotions: We are often aware of being angry, but we are less aware of what emotions lurk behind that anger. Typically, anger is a reaction to hurt, sadness, rejection, or other painful emotions. It's OK to tell someone you feel angry, but it's much more helpful if you understand why.

Consider other perspectives: Most people don't intentionally try to hurt you, especially those

227

who care about you. We more often unintentionally hurt the people we care about or retaliate for being hurt. The initial reaction of anger is almost always self-centered, reflecting a belief such as, *"She shouldn't have done that to me; she's a horrible person."*

If you can cool off and obtain a broader perspective, you will often find that whatever made you angry was unintentional, or you set the ball rolling through your behavior. You might not like it, but you must act compassionately and honestly to review your mistakes. Find a broader perspective; it will help you not take things so personally.

Communicate: When you've cooled down, identified your emotions, and considered things from the other person's perspective (possibly with the help of a peer), then you talk to the other person about why you're angry. If you tend to avoid conflict, you might be tempted to let it go – and sometimes you should – but communicating will

228

improve your relationships and help keep resentments from festering. Focus on your feelings and avoid accusations; this is often difficult, but it gets easier with practice.

Please write it down: It might help to write down whatever you're angry about. However, this should be a short list because it will only reinforce your resentments if long. Describe the situation accurately and clearly articulate your emotions and behavior.

On an esoteric level, the fiery part of Fire represents the indescribable nature of our source – Toa / God. God is not a destination but a way to it that will never meet its goal. The fiery part of Fire can only be understood in one personal God. My seventh-dimensional godhead directs this personal God to direct us along the path.

These godheads open new chapters in human life with needed experiences offered. Some of these

229

experiences might seem backward, but they open us up to different experiences apart from innovations. These godheads monitor the riddle of who God is in the most creative way for us.

To perform this Fire of fire magic/meditation, you lay out your altar like the rest in this series but use the blue dot in its center. Chant *Agni/Vayu* four times and twice daily until your candle burns out. Your Mind will be enlightened to all new ideas and ways of living, and you will gain answers to the most mysterious of your soul's questions.

Agni Vayu, or the Airy part of Fire

A field of green symbolizes the airy part of the Fire with an upward red triangle and a blue dot in the center of that red triangle. The natural symbol is nature is our Fire of Mind. Like the fiery part of Fire, its symbol in nature is theoretical and cannot be depicted as a physical symbol. An old friend of mine, who is very psychic, Michael, was the first person to indicate to me that this symbol is the Ego. He was a high priest in an Egyptian lodge I was in many years ago in New York City in my youth. Now, I use my skill of *Spirit Writing* – automatic writing to delineate the various Tattva.

The Fire of Mind can be described in many ways. I will delineate a few of them for you. A new aged author named Alice Bailey wrote that the soul is an Ego. When most people would write of the word – soul, she would write of the word – Ego instead. So, I wonder, what connection does the Ego

have with the soul? According to the new aged book
– *A Course in Miracles*, the Ego represents - our split from God and separation from His reality.

So, between the two New Aged authors, we understand that the Ego/Soul represents our independence from our source – God, and the need for the Fire of Mind; this was how we gained our consciousness - the fiery part of Fire or Agni Agni. It is odd how consciousness and anger seem to go hand and hand. I guess what we are truly angry at, is the nightmare of a world that we have created in our falls from grace with God. Our fall is made complete in this Tattva of the Ego/Soul/ fire of Mind. Perhaps we were angry because we thought that God was hiding something from us without the independent consciousness we have obtained for ourselves. This Fire of Mind is our declaration of independence from our source.

Other sources say that the Souls embody misunderstandings with the physical planes. We

232

have no idea what we got involved in with our split from God. We found ourselves in the dark, and this Fire was our only guiding light.

This is the true knowledge of Agni - Vayu brings out the true and accurate knowledge of what Agni is! Now, according to Agni Agni, any words that might express the nature of Agni are all false representations put into words. I heard it being said that words are just symbols or are far from any descriptions of reality. So, is it inaccurate to claim that this Tattva, the airy part of Fire, can describe the truth of God's true nature?

The understanding is that the fire element represents a personal God and not the one and only God - our true source. So, any descriptions that the Vayu element can only depict our personal Gods in exile here in this dream of separation from the real God – our source. Only in the Akasha Vayu do we gain a better knowledge of the nature of God – our

233

source – not in Agni, which only holds the knowledge of a personal God we chose to possess.

You might wonder, is all lost in this case? The answer is No! The Earth element Prithvi directly relates to Akasha – the Holy Spirit of God through Vayu – the Air element. This connection enriches the Earth's element to heal and house Godly energies to balance and stabilize our wayward souls. One can be lost to God in this bad dream and at one with Him simultaneously. These energies are built into the Prithvi - Earth element. In our common speech, we call it grounding.

To my knowledge, the best way to ground one's self is to work hard at what you do here on Earth. There is a Greek God whose mother is Gaia named Amateurs. He would challenge all passers-by to wrestling matches and remain invincible if he remained in contact with his mother - the Earth. As Greek wrestling, like its modern equivalent, typically attempted to force opponents to the

234

ground, Antaeus always won, killing his opponents. He built a temple for his father, the sea god Poseidon, using their skulls. Amateurs fought Heracles as he was on his way to the Garden of Hesperides to perform his eleventh Labor. Heracles realized that he could not beat Amateurs by throwing or pinning him. Instead, he held him aloft in the air and then crushed him to death in a bear hug.

The above passage shows a connection we all have to the Earth. The Earth is our strength and means of life; we cannot live apart from Earth. Akasha infuses Prithvi, The Earth, has divine energies for maintaining our lives. We live on holy grounds here; our home planet is negatively charged like we are. Akasha is positively charged as it reaches us. Akasha's true nature is neutral and an element that is divine and very hard to describe. I will try my best in that future chapter to describe it.

235

It is best for us to work with our planet's energies and humanity in order to gain the positive charges that we need. So, this positively charged Akasha creates a neutral field when contacting our world and us; this neutral field is a vacuum for the objective, neutrally divine Akasha to generate further and maintain life on our planet. The second envelope of Akasha is what makes our Earth's element divine. The first envelope creates a neutral field to house the divine Akasha, which is beyond words to describe. I will use poetry and mythology to depict its nature when I write about Akasha Akasha.

So, when Vayu influences Agni, as in this Tattva, we can see the most genuine nature of Agni-Fire. This nature of the personal God guides us like a sacred flame – Th Goddess – Vesta. The sacred Fire of Vesta was a sacred eternal flame in ancient Rome. The Vestal Virgins, originally numbering two, later four, and eventually, six, were selected by lot and served for thirty years, tending the holy Fire and performing other rituals connected to domestic life —among them was the ritual sweeping of the temple on June 15 and the preparation of food for specific festivals.

As you can see, this sacred flame has a feminine and domestic nature. The home is the core of our existence. Maintaining a clean and organized home is essential for the divine energies of God to be with you. Being a good cook and preparing fine meals for your family is a part of its divine nature as well.

You thought I could have written something of a progressive nature to this connection of the divine and our planet but NO! You see, there is not much that our Earth's mother cares to prepare for but to have a clean and happy home life. She – Gaia doesn't care much about the technologies of humanity and sending men to the Moon or Mars. She – Gaia, our Earth mother, preferred us more when we did not harm nature but lived along with it instead. We will surely advance technologically and live in our elevated cities above the Earth. Our planet will also return to its natural wonder with the animal and fish kingdoms in its own time.

Above all else, we can technologically advance as much as we care to, but we must maintain the family unit to be grounded on the Earth. Family life is highly regarded in the Mormon faith. Family life is the grounding of our sacred flames upon the Earth. Even if we are in our future elevated cities, we will still experience this grounding in them.

So, utilizing what I have written, our personal God would be a domesticated one of the family unit. A healthy family life is essential for our growth. Neglect and child abuse are counterproductive to the development of our families. If God himself were to speak to us and ask how we can please Him, His will for us would make us happy, clean, and productive families for our best growth. The truth is that nothing else is expected of us.

The Christ, the Buddha, and all the Upanishads were only misdirecting us away from the true essentials in life for us on planet Earth. Yes, what they had to say was all wonderful and quite helpful, but not in line with what is expected of us to live on our planet – Earth.

Are you possibly shocked to read that a successful life on our planet can be obtained in such a simple manner? Yes, the family unit and good housekeeping is the main thing that is expected of us for a successful life. The Mormon faith does have issues with its one hundred billion dollars in its investments account named - Ensign Peak, established in the early 1960s and has a tax exemption.

This religion preaches of a second coming of Jesus Christ after many world wars and the loss of

239

our money system. Who knows if they are correct, but many of their church officials say they can help many people with their money rather than just hording it.

One last thing I can mention about this Tattva of the airy part of Fire is that it's the knowledge of our personal God. We see this in our religious books like the so-called - Holy Bible, the Book of Mormon, the Upanishads, the Tibetan Book of the Dead, or whatever New Age material you might find are all that we have come up with regarding our personal gods.

Now, in the light of the truth of the Tattva Agni Agni – the fiery part of Fire, all these books are just man's perceptions of the divine and not the Divine itself! I ask you now to take them all with a grain of salt and focus on your home life instead. Yes, in the seventh-dimensional worlds, we have gods walking amongst men; they help us with the riddle we must try to solve or give up as being

240

ridiculous; they may serve as personal gods for us if we are sincere enough at heart; they can be quite helpful to us and all of mankind.

In conclusion, consciousness is a reaction of Agni Angi and Agni Vayu together. Yes, our eyes with our vision did have a fracture in this, but the ability to self-analyze who you are and who God is for humanity to perform. Only at the human level can we do this. Only for humans upon our planet Earth can we truly understand who God is higher than our space brothers; this will come in due time – be patient and incarnate to this planet exclusively.

The family unit and cleanliness have a lot to do with the knowledge of God for us to realize. A family's proper living situation will be taught as humanity evolves. We will raise finer children to adults then. So many people turn to crime because of a poor example left to them in their childhood by depressed adults.

241

Finally, regarding this Tattva that spirituality will be illuminated in your Minds. When I was in the army, I was very depressed and isolated. After my release, I was illuminated by everything regarding the New Age movement; this did get out of hand when I would talk about God and the New Age banter at work- I was seen as spacey. Yes, even nuns in medieval convents were seen as spacey if they had revelations from prayer. This spaciness is the akasha working through Agni – fire in our Minds – it can be a bit ungrounding at first.

Back to spirituality, humanity needs an incarnation of Vishnu to illuminate our Minds and heart from time to time. Saint Francis came when the church was seen to be as cold as the stones it was built with. Oddly, Saint Francis was ever so humble to have his church and grounds be made into one of Italy's finest museums of art and culture. Though, he did establish his brotherhood when he was living. The Franciscan order is still a brotherhood to his day.

So, whatever spirituality you choose, it is best to make you love all mankind regardless of race, sexuality, or nationality and to be a good and honest person overall. We all must obey the laws and pay our fair share of taxes. It is selfish that the rich people and rich companies use excess loops to pay very little taxes when the middle classes pay a much higher percentage of taxes than the rich. The USA must establish a new taxation system that makes it fair for all, regardless of income. We all must pay the same percentage in taxes.

To perform this magic/meditation, one gets the same green tablecloths and a red candle. You draw a red upward triangle on it with a blue dot in the center of that. You then chant the words – *Agni Vayu* four times twice daily until the red candle burns out. If done right, you will consciously gain the right understanding of Agni – Fire. Your Mind

243

will be illuminated with the truth of God that is right
for you,   at your present level of growth.

Agni Akasha, or the Aetheric part of Fire

The aetheric part of Fire symbol is a green field with a red upward triangle in its center with a purple egg in the center of that triangle. It has no symbol in nature as it is aetheric. One thing about it is that it rescues our so-called personal gods and allows them to serve us as if they were real Gods to us; this is an act of grace by the hands of divinity alone. Divinity understands that we need these so-called Gods for our growth, but they can also hold us back. This saving act is totally out of compassion by our real and living God.

Our saviors that come to our world are all blessed by this aetheric part of fire - Agni Akasha - to help us in our darkest hours. However, they might speak of something other than Gaia's regiment for us - good housekeeping and family life. Is her message more universal than that? Our Earth Mother – Gaia, doesn't expect much of us. She is not

245

truly that interested in us. Gaia is interested in animal, fish, and plant life. She does not mind having us because we evolved from the animal kingdom – the apes. She is not that involved in our progression apart from the basics in life – home and family. If it were up to her, we would not even be here.

She loved having the dinosaurs around. You can see that in their very long history in our world. The age of the dinosaurs on Earth was between 165 and 177 million years. During the Triassic period, they first appeared between 243 and 231 million years ago. Dinosaurs became extinct around 66 million years ago; this means they were on Earth for far longer than they've been extinct. The fury mammals started about 66 million years ago. They developed on land and seas to be what they are today.

The first human ancestors appeared between five million and seven million years ago, probably

246

when some African apelike creatures began to walk habitually on two legs. They used flakes of crude stone tools 2.5 million years ago. Then some spread from Africa into Asia and Europe two million years ago. The biological and social evolution of early humans whether it started 400,000 or 2 million years ago when they made use of fire to cook their meats and vegetables. Humanity arranged themselves in colonies about that same time.

As you can see, humanity is just a recent development from the animal kingdom. For the most part, Gaia was more interested in animal, fish, and plant life and not the development of humanity, though she does have some consideration for us. However, Gaia does not expect much from us. Her concerns are other things besides us.

So, our saviors did not align with our Earth mother's ideals. The overhead supervision for them to come was out of the hands of Gaia, but she permitted it just the same. That happened because

247

Gaia is seen as not doing enough to help us as a human race by the universal lords - they need to intervene from time to time.

We are under the leadership of the seven Kumaras of Tibet. That kingdom or world is called – Shamballa. Shamballa is of a finer grain of the Earth element than we are, and is seen as aetheric. The inhabitants there are still physical, but they resemble astral entities; they are what we call – Angels; they have come to us in our many hours of need.

This world of theirs also has a black hand to them. These black hands are mentioned in the Bible as the *"Lords of the air"* The two forces greatly influence our daily lives. Overall, the good forces will have their day with us and construct a healthy and advanced society. The seven lords of Shamballa have human representatives with us all. These representatives are what we call – the Illuminati.

The seven or eight listed Kumaras in the Mahabharata, a total of seven youths: 1) Aniruddha, 2) Sana, 3) Sanatsujata, 4) Sanaka, 5) Sanandana, 6) Sanat kumara, 7) Kapila, and 8) Sanatana and further mentions that "Knowledge comes to these seven rishis, of itself (without being dependent on study or exertion). Sanat Kumara is the leader of the seven Kumaras.

Each Kumara in charge is a particular aspect of life here on Earth. The seven or eight Kumaras were created out of the Mind of the Lord Brahman to serve his creations. They refused to choose a higher path. Brahman got angry and made Lord Shiva correct them. Brahman chose to address the Lord Vishnu. Vishnu responded by creating four Kumaras to serve Brahman's creations - Sanaka, Sanandana, Sanatana, and Sanatkumara. I did not list a few twice; I just listed all of them – the original Kumaras were just four disobedient ones who later

249

decided to serve Father Brahman and all of mankind.

The seven lords of Shamballa seem to pick up where our Earth Mother Gaia cannot help us. Our Earth's mother is not only schooled in human developments but also animal, fish, and plant life. However, she gives Shamballa the authority to develop us in her absence. The main lord of Shamballa is Sanat Kumara, or the *great lord of eternal youth.*

According to the post-1900 publications of theosophy, **Sanat Kumara** is an "Advanced Being" at the Cosmic level of initiation, which in his regard is the "Lord" or "Regent" of Earth and humanity. He heads the Spiritual Hierarchy of Earth, who dwells in Shambhala (also known as 'The City of Enoch'). According to the adherents to the Ascended Master Teachings, Shambhala is a floating city manifested on the aetheric plane somewhere above the Gobi Desert in the borderlands of Mongolia. Sanat

250

Kumara is a mythical religious figure often referred to as an advanced human master with a consciousness far evolved from a human master as a master human is born of mankind.

His consciousness, age, and experience of cosmic and interplanetary life as well as deity, far exceed that of a human master. He is depicted as a young man who does not ever age. The Sanskrit name Sanat Kumara means "always a youth." He is the most prominent of the Kumaras. In Hinduism, Sanat Kumara is sometimes called Skanda, or Karthikeya the son of Shiva and Parvati. Karthikeya is the God of war and commander-in-chief of the divine army of the gods.

There was a time when human life in this world was in question. The planetary Logi of Venus interrupted our normal process of evolution that Gaia approved of. We were not to understand the forces of good and evil as they did on planet Venus. This change of destiny put human life in jeopardy.

251

Sanat Kumar stepped in to save humanity millions of years ago. Due to that disruption of our future, our Earth mother was even less interested in us as a race. She was not herself schooled in the understanding of good and evil. To the Venusians, they called our planet- the dark lotus virgin.

They said that the planet Earth held the mysteries of all life in our Universe. To understand being human is to understand the whole Universe; this is true since our planet Earth and our Universe vibrate at the exact hertz of 432 HZ. Our Earth Mother Gaia planned to reveal these mysteries as we developed as a race. However, due to the change in destiny, she could no longer instruct us, being that she did not know good and evil. She felt that both home and family values were enough.

However, when the correction is made, and good and evil are thought of on our planet, Gaia will open her mysteries to mankind.

One more thing is the Gnostic faith. The Gnostics believe in the Universe of wisdom or – *Sophia*. Since the 432 Hz of our planet is the same as the Universe and what the Venusians call our planet – the black lotus virgin, we can see that both are goddesses. Our earth mother is a goddess too, and she will impart to us Sophia - wisdom through her agents in due time. It is interesting that the Gnostic faith came very close to revealing such divine Knowledge to humanity. The Catholic Church saw Gnosticism as a threat and protested it out of existence. The faith only renumbered, employing the New Age movement 50 years ago or more as a faith.

In Theosophy, Maitreya, or Lord Maitreya, in Sanskrit, the word maitrī "friendship," is an advanced spiritual entity and high-ranking member of a reputed hidden spiritual hierarchy, the Masters of the Ancient Wisdom. Lord Maitreya is lord over our planet, like Lucifer, who was lord over the

253

planet Venus. Now, it is up to Lord Maitreya to rectify our destiny by teaching us the mysteries of the Universe. Our Earth mother, Gaia, has chosen to work through him on this matter of teaching. Life on Earth was never meant to be so violent or with such diversities of knowing good and evil. Under his name, the lord Maitreya is a friend to humanity. He presided over the Illuminati and directed human affairs under the guidance of the seven Kumara of Shamballa.

The understanding is that the blessings of our personal God will be enough, and the so-called - holy books are second-rate to the truth of God that is beyond any words. The oriental esoteric book, The Hua Hu Ching, by Hua Ching Ni describes that God is beyond any words a man should write about Him, and God is the unknowable and unspeakable.

So, any of these prophets of old with their teachers are just here under the hospice of mercy by the divine as a tangible means our human mind can

254

grasp onto; apart from that – they all should be taken with a grain of salt.

This mercy seems like a contradiction to the instructions of Agni Agni – the fiery part of fire, but our human minds need to grasp something left-brain oriented. A brain that is only ten pounds of flesh understands the intangible. However, it is our human nature to want to have a concrete understanding of God.

Divinity knows of this and has outstretched its hand to us employing the Aetheric part of Agni - Agni Akasha. Our personal gods do serve us, but they need uplifting as well. If I did not explain what a personal god is, it's our mind's take on what God's nature is about. My seventh-dimensional godhead supervises such interpretation, if such can be used constructively.

Since it is only a – take, it needs to be spiritually reoriented to serve us better. Both the seventh and tenth lords are here to help us. The tenth-dimensional Lords cannot reach us; they affect us through their magic indirectly – the seventh-dimensional lords directly affect us.

Our Lady of Guadalupe (Spanish: *Nuestra Señora de Guadalupe*), also known as the Virgin of Guadalupe (Spanish: *Virgen de Guadalupe*), is a Catholic title of Mary, mother of Jesus associated with a series of five Marian apparitions, which we believe to have occurred in December 1531, and a venerated image on a cloak enshrined within the Basilica of Our Lady of Guadalupe in Mexico City.

The basilica is the most-visited Catholic shrine in the world and the world's third most-visited sacred site. This is just one outreach of divinity to inspire mankind. There are numerous cases when divinity has stretched its hand out to us. We seem to be encouraged by these miraculous occurrences in our human history. We build buildings and religions around physical and aetheric individuals, like the Virgin of Guadalupe. It seems to be well stated that our human psyches need these divine signs from above to inspire us in our darkest times.

St Francis of Assisi, Italian San Francesco d' Assisi, baptized Giovanni, renamed Francesco, in full Francesco di Pietro di Bernardone. He was (born 1181/82, in Assisi, duchy of Spoleto [Italy]—died October 3, 1226, in Assisi. Francis canonized on July 16, 1228, feast day October 4). He founded the Franciscan orders of the Friars Minor (Ordo Fratrum Minorum), the women's Order of St. Clare (the Poor Clares), and the Third lay Order.

He was also head of a movement for evangelical poverty in the early 13th century. His evangelical zeal, consecration to poverty, charity, and personal charisma drew thousands of followers. Francis's devotion to the human Jesus and his desire to follow Jesus' example reflected and reinforced essential developments in medieval spirituality.

The Poverello ("Poor Little Man") is one of the most revered religious figures in Roman Catholic history, and he and St. Catherine of Siena are the patron saints of Italy. In 1979 Pope John Paul II recognized him as the patron saint of ecology. St Francis was one of many notaries of the Catholic Church who came in our darkest hours. St Francis came when the church appeared as a cold, unfriendly, and hard-authoritative institution to the Italian people. The saint brought new life to the church and lives of the Catholics. Unfortunately, Assisi became one of Italy's capitals of the high arts in Italy and the world.

I have read that whenever evil presides upon the Earth, Lord Vishnu will be there to rectify the light back to Earth; this is the divinity of the aetheric element of Akasha. We will go into greater detail in the chapters to come.

258

Now, to perform this magic, it is like the others in the Agni series but in the middle of the red triangle, draw a purple or black egg – chant *Agni Akasha* four times twice a day and open yourselves to the mercy of a righteous personal God to help you on your path.

If this magic is done right, you will be drawn to mystical poetry and stories that house abstract concepts like the strange symbology used by the medieval alchemist of ancient times. Yes, odd, and unusual symbols will be presented to you. They will open you up to an all-new world of wonder. However, it is undesirable with no words or visions that are the best to attract; they will help you the most. You can even do this by practicing Zazen mediation.

Vayu – Air

Vayu Tattva or an Orange Field with a Large Blue Dot

Vayu is the God of air/wind. He is also considered the God of life, as air is vital to being alive. Like other gods, he is considered a fighter, destroyer, powerful and heroic. He is the father of Hanuman, known as Pavan Putra (son of Pavana). It is believed that Vayu was Iranian roots worshipped under the same name – Vayu.

The element of Air - Vayu Tattva symbol is an orange field and a large blue dot in its center. The orange field represents the spirit as it resembles gold, and the blue dot represents the spirit's individuality.

So, we have a divine union of all spirits and a separation of the individuality of the spirit - You might wonder, how can this be? The answer is that individuality is an illusion and that we all are at one with the divine. So, in this case, this Tattva represents the split from our source and the illusion that there was a split.

The symbol in nature of this Tattva is the winds and the Mind! These winds are forever changeable and never at rest like our Mind; this restlessness is also a characteristic of this Tattva: it is restless in its contradiction to its character of being at one with all and being split simultaneously. The winds of the world are seen to follow both hot and cold impressions to create high and low pressures to control the weather. These opposites are what I have mentioned in the oneness and the split from our source. In this way, the weather is another physical symbol for this Tattva. In this way, it represents the split – Mind as well.

Our Minds are truly split into two parts – the left and right lobes. The left side is our rational thinking, and the right is our irrational thinking. In humans, the lobes of the brain are divided by several bumps and grooves. These are gyri (bumps) and sulci (grooves or fissures). The folding of the brain, which results from both gyri and sulci, increases its surface area and enables more cerebral cortex matter to fit inside the skull. Depending on the person, one can use mostly one side over the other. Artists use their right brains more, while analytical types use their left brains; *they are meant* to work together as one for the best thinking possible.

What causes thinking in the brain? It is when neurons (brain cells) release brain chemicals, known as neurotransmitters, which generate these electrical signals in neighboring neurons. The electrical signals propagate like a wave to thousands of neurons, which leads to thought formation.

One theory explains that thoughts are generated when neurons fire. This firing of the neurons is controlled by an Aetheric brain called – The Mind. This Aetheric works like a hologram, and it is intangible to physical examinations as it

263

exists in the non-physical – only the fleshy brain is tangible to such investigations – the Mind is not!

Referring to our source, God, in the truest sense, we have never left our source – God. We are all with Him now! It is just a dream that we fell into, a dream that was corrected the moment it happened. In that creation of that moment, we created time itself to understand what happened and why it happened – the dream of separation.

At that moment – the blue dot appeared as the individual spirit entity. This phenomenon occurred as we fell into this bizarre world of duality where the light of God – His divine sons defused themselves into an infinite amount of individual spirit entities that are without number. So, we are now in this dream of separation.

However, we can still be of the higher Mind's attitude that we are at one with our source by accepting His peace. Accepting the peace of God is a representation of our one-ness with Him. I ask you all to accept this peace now in your lives. If you could do this, the Mind's lousy weather will improve.

For that fact, what do we call – the Mind? We must first clarify what most folks mean when using the term "Mind." What exactly are they referring to? In common parlance, the Mind most often refers to the seat of human consciousness, the thinking, and feeling that seems to be an agentic causal force that is somehow related but is also seemingly separable from the body. The idea of life after death is intuitively plausible to many, because our mental life seems so different from our bodies that we could imagine our souls existing long after decomposing; this leads to a commonsense dualism that is part and parcel of many religious worldviews.

The UT – micro liter suggests some semantic problems referring to the human self-consciousness system as "the Mind." One reason for this, has to do

265

with what Freud "discovered" over a century ago and is now well-known by modern-day psychologists (see, e.g., Tim Wilson's Strangers to Us) — consciousness is only a small portion of mental processes. Consciousness and Mind are thus not synonymous. We must then realize that the problem is either in the consciousness-brain-body system or the consciousness-mind-brain-body system.

Recognizing the need to separate the Mind from consciousness is one of the keys to resolving the issues. *What, then, is the relationship between Mind and consciousness?* The UT tells us we can turn to the cognitive revolution in psychology to ground our answer. The mental process was birthed as a mixture of work on information theory, artificial intelligence, and cybernetics. It gave rise to the computational theory of the Mind, which offers a solution to a big piece of the puzzle. The computational theory of the Mind posits that the nervous system is an information-processing system. It translates changes in the body and the environment into a language of neural impulses representing the animal-environment relationship.

The computational theory of the Mind was a huge breakthrough because it allows us, for the first time, to separate the Mind from the brain-body conceptually. How?

The way to do this is we can now conceive of - the Mind as the flow of information through the nervous system, this flow of information can be conceptually separated from the biophysical matter that makes up the nervous system. To see how we can consider the separation of the information from the actual nervous system itself, think of a book.

The book's mass, temperature, and other physical Dimensions can now be considered as roughly akin to the brain. Then think about the information content (i.e., the story the book tells or

267

claims it makes). In computational theory which is akin to the Mind. The Mind, then, is the information instantiated and processed by the nervous system.

Although the cognitive revolution was a great move forward, problems emerged. This was in part because now that the Mind could be conceptually separated from the brain with relative ease, researchers became fascinated with models of disembodied or artificial algorithmic processors that had little connection with the other elements of mental phenomena, such as conscious experience, culture, overt behavior, or the brain.

The problem was that these models were far removed from the human mind-brain system. With its macro-level view and capacity to assimilate and integrate critical perspectives, the UT allows us to build off the cognitive revolution's central insight and connect it back to the brain, evolution, human action/behavioral science, and culture.

268

To my research, the human brain is dead and lifeless; it is reactionary to the Mind, which is immaterial. What the Mind is needs to be discovered. Consciousness is the firing of the brain, but the Mind is beyond consciousness and of a realm all to its own. That is why we can gain heavenly inspiration. The brain's consciousness can only direct us through a room but not to God – this is a matter beyond the brain into a super-consciousness unknown to mankind currently.

As far as the physical properties of Air: Air is considered a "pure" element, but in fact, the air that's all around us is made up of a variety of gases: primarily Nitrogen and Oxygen, with almost 1% Argon and even smaller amounts of Carbon dioxide and other elements such as Krypton and Helium. The composition of air is just suitable for life on Earth, though. The amount of oxygen has changed throughout Earth's very long history. When the dinosaurs were around millions of years ago in

269

Pangea, the world had very little oxygen due to the dryness of the world. The world back then was a desert. Due to low green plant life, oxygen was relatively low. There were times when the world was tropical, and the oxygen level was relatively high.

Doing air Vayu magic by casting Air stars can cause many friends to communicate with you. In his book, "The Golden Dawn", Alister Crawley has instructions for casting in and banishing out the four elements. I recommend the works of Crawley as a good start in the occult if you feel that is your path.

According to this book on Tattva, you put down an orange table covered with a blue candle. Draw a large blue dot on the candle's glass and chant *Vayu* four times twice a day until the blue candle burns out. Remember your wish for communication between you and that particular person or persons.

270

Air is one of our sources of life here on Earth. Life would not be possible without this element. Oxygen enriches our red blood cells and makes them red. The oxygen is brought to all areas of the bodies of both man and all other mammals, including fish, for their survival. We all need oxygen, water, and food to survive on Earth. On other planets - who knows what is needed for survival? We still need to find out.

Breathing and following your breath is quite important in many forms of meditation. Both in Hindu and Buddhist meditation, one follows their breath. I do encourage you to meditate and learn to follow your breath. My personal mediation ignites a colossal burst of energy. It involves stillness of the Mind and body to the point of not breathing or listening to anything. I can only do this for a few seconds at a time; however, it is very effective.

The breathing meditation is called - the second death. I try to practice it from time to time.

271

This breathing meditation is quite advanced, and hard for most new people to meditate. It might be better to start by following your breath upright on the floor in a group.

Vayu Prithvi, or the
Earthly part of Air

The earthy part of Air symbolizes an orange field and a large blue dot in its center with a yellow square. It represents the air element made physical in the oxygen we all breathe; this is the realm of the grounded Mind, and it rules practical thinking. In this way, it rules left-brained rational thinking; this is the analytical brain.

The type of brain usage is also in the frontal lobes. The frontal lobes are essential for voluntary movement, expressive language, and managing higher-level executive functions. Executive functions refer to a collection of cognitive skills, including the capacity to plan, organize, initiate, self-monitor, and control one's responses to achieve a goal.

Math and engineering are fine examples of this Tattva. Only the higher forms of this expression seem right brained or irrational. However, if it can

273

be expressed on paper or with a computer, it is left-brained thinking. We use math every day in our culture. We would only change today's society with math and engineering. The use of measurements and sizes is akin to this Tattva. All four of these studies have in common that their findings are put right in your hand, with no doubts that the results are all finite.

What is finite can be described as:

- having definite or definable limits.

Such as, a *finite* number of possibilities.

- having a limited nature or existence.

Such as, finite beings

- completely determinable in theory or in fact by counting, measurement, or thought.

Such as, the *finite* velocity of light

- less than an arbitrary positive integer and more significant than the negative of that integer

- having a finite number of elements.

  Such as, a *finite* set

- of, relating to, or being a verb or verb form
  that can function as a predicate or as the
  initial element of one and that is limited (as
  in tense, person, and number)

Such as, finite verbs like "is" and "are."

The above statements are the grasp of the finite left brain. We are not even talking about the Mind here. The Mind is eight-dimensional and far outside the confines of our left brain's finite thought processes. The rationale of the eight-dimensional Mind supersedes our lower Mind's – the physical brain's scope of the perception of itself and life in general.

Sound waves of all kinds are akin to this Tattva. That fact is that it's crystallized Air. Air is constantly in motion and creating ripples. When these waves physically affect you – we have sound or the earthly part of air Vayu Prithvi.

How are sound waves created? In physics, sound is a vibration propagating as an acoustic wave through a transmission medium such as a gas, liquid, or solid. In human physiology and psychology, sound is the *reception* of such waves and their *perception* by the brain. Only acoustic waves with frequencies between 20 Hz and 20 kHz, the audio frequency range, elicit an auditory perception in humans.

Air at atmospheric pressure represents sound waves with wavelengths of 17 meters (56 ft) to 1.7 centimeters (0.67 in). Sound waves above 20 kHz are known as ultrasound and are not audible to humans. Sound waves below 20 Hz are known as infrasound. Different animal species have varying hearing ranges.

Sound is defined as "(a) Oscillation in pressure, stress, particle displacement, particle

276

velocity, etc., propagated in a medium with internal forces (e.g., elastic or viscous), or the superposition of such propagated oscillation. (b) Auditory sensation evoked by the oscillation described in (a)." Sound can be viewed as a wave motion in Air or other elastic media. In this case, sound is a stimulus. Sound can also be viewed as an excitation of the hearing mechanism that results in the perception of sound. In this case, sound is a sensation.

The physical part of Air creates the pressure needed for sound waves to be created. I have read that the OM sound made things physical and non-physical.

The mighty Om can be described as the following: *Om* (or *Aum*) (Sanskrit: ॐ, ओम्, romanized: *Ōṃ*) is a sacred sound, syllable, mantra, or invocation in Hinduism. *Om* is the prime symbol of Hinduism. It is said to be the essence of the

supreme Absolute consciousness, *Atman,
Brahman,* or the cosmic world.

In Indic traditions, *Om* serves as a sonic representation of the divine, a standard of Vedic authority, and a central aspect of soteriological doctrines and practices. The syllable is often found at the beginning and the end of chapters in the Vedas, the Upanishads, and other Hindu texts.

Om emerged in the Vedic corpus and is said to be an encapsulated form of *Samavedic* chants or songs. It is a sacred spiritual incantation made before and during the recitation of spiritual texts, during *puja* and private prayers, in ceremonies of rites of passage (*samskara*) such as weddings, and during meditative and spiritual activities such as Pranava yoga. It is part of the iconography found in ancient and medieval-era manuscripts, temples, monasteries, and spiritual retreats in Hinduism, Buddhism, Jainism, and Sikhism.

As a syllable, it is often chanted independently or before a spiritual recitation and during meditation in Hinduism, Buddhism, and Jainism. The syllable *Oum* is also called **Onkara Omkara** and **Pranava,** among many other names.

Five things to know about the OM.

Om is the primordial sound of the universe. Heard in temples, yoga studios, households, and even television and movies, the chanting and symbol of Om is familiar to most as it has permeated the Western world since the counterculture of the 1960s.

While to the layperson, it's synonymous with meditation and seen simply as a doorway to tranquility for yogic practitioners, the true meaning of Om is deeply embedded in Hindu philosophy. To comprehend its truly profound effects, one must have a basic understanding of sound.

Though many comprehend sound as something to be heard, its mechanism is a little more

279

complex. Sound is made up of vibrations. These vibrations are produced from a source, travel through the Air, and then are picked up by the ear before being interpreted by the brain, which assigns them some value. The number of vibrations per second is known as frequency. Because all matter is composed of atomic material in constant motion, everything, and everyone vibrates at some frequency.

The great inventor and scientist Nikola Tesla once said, "If you want to find the secrets of the universe, think in terms of energy, frequency, and vibration."

The Word Om is defined by Hindu scripture as being the primordial sound of creation. It is the original vibration of the universe. From this first vibration, all other vibrations can manifest.

Why Meditate on Om

It is well-substantiated that sound vibration significantly impacts a person's physical, emotional, and mental state. By chanting Om, we can align our frequency with the original universal frequency, which is essential in spiritual practice. As an iron rod becomes as hot as fire when it encounters flames, a person can spiritualize their life by staying in connection with the spiritual energy of the Absolute.

Om is the seed of ethereal sound; through transcendental sound one can transform the Mind and the senses. By chanting Om, the Mind becomes aligned with the breath, which enables a person to get into an elevated state of consciousness called *samadhi*.

The activity of attaining *samadhi* brings the materially absorbed Mind under control, which allows a person to have a one-pointed focus toward spiritual realization because the Absolute is beyond the understanding of the ordinary material senses, spiritualizing the Mind — the center of all sensual activities, through sound vibration is necessary to set in motion the process of transcendental realization. Like a majestic tree that can be generated from a tiny seed, the glorious tree of spirituality can grow from the sincere chanting of Om.

Symbolism of Om

While its symbol is recognized by most, much fewer know what the combination of curves, crescents, and dots, which make up Om's visual representation, truly stands for. Each aspect of the visual form of Om signifies a particular state of reality. The large lower curve marks the normal waking state (*jāgrat*). In this condition, the Mind identifies with the physical body and perceives the world through the senses.

The upper curve indicates the unconscious state or that of deep sleep (*sushupti;* This is a state of total unawareness in which you are in a deep, dreamless sleep and withdrawn from both physical and mental activities).

The middle curve denotes the dream state (*swapna*). The dream state is between deep sleep and waking, where a person explores the subconscious. Your consciousness is turned inwards as your fears, hopes, and desires manifest themselves in an imaginary world.

The dot is a symbol of enlightenment (*turiyā*). In this state, a person becomes harmonized with the Absolute, recognizing that all creation is made up of spirit and is united through that commonality. This state is beyond the ordinary senses and can only be achieved by associating with spiritual energy.

The crescent represents *Maya*, which separates the three curves from the dot. Maya is the illusion that binds an individual soul to the material world. One can transcend the three curves of material consciousness by chanting Om and attaining the dot of enlightenment.

Universal Access of Om

Like an object depicted in numerous ways by numerous painters, Om's essence is uniquely manifested and accessed by different types of people worldwide. As yogis commonly conclude their meditations with the chanting of Om, the Judeo-Christian utterance of "Amen," and the Islamic version "Amin," is used by followers to evoke the energy of the Divine at the end of a prayer.

Even within Hinduism, the meaning and connotations of Om are perceived in various ways. Though heard and often written as "Om," due to the way it sounds when it is repeatedly chanted, the sacred syllable is originally and more accurately spelled as "aum." Broken down, the three letters of A – U – M represent several sacred trinities: · The different conditions of consciousness — the waking, the dreaming, and the deep sleep state. Brahma, Vishnu, and Shiva are the deities in charge of the universe's creation, preservation, and destruction.

- The three original Vedic scriptures — Rg, Yajur, and Sāma.
- The three worlds — earth, atmosphere, and oceans/ether.
- The three aspects of time — past, present, and future.

In the Bhakti tradition (yoga of devotion) — Krishna (seen by his devotees as the God of Creation), Rādhārāni (Krishna's eternal consort, or God's female counterpart), and the ordinary living beings. Om encompasses all creation, and anyone who seeks it can attain its merciful energy regardless of who they are, where they come from, or whichever faith they follow.

How to Chant Om

285

Though there are no hard and fast rules for chanting Om, understanding the fundamental techniques of producing its sound can help provide a foundation to better connect to the Divine. As explained earlier, Om represents the universe's creation, preservation, and dissolution.

The seven main chakras — wheels of energy in the body relating to the physical, psychological, and spiritual aspects of our lives, provide a path through which the sound of Om begins, passes through, and eventually dissolves itself.

After taking a deep breath, Om (Aum) chanting starts at the solar plexus chakra, near the diaphragm, where the "A" of the syllable is emphasized. As the sound progresses, "U" sustains the mantra through the heart, throat, and third eye chakras until it reaches the crown. The sound dissolves at the crown chakra, at which point the mantra has developed into its last part, the "M."

286

Finding a quiet place to focus without being disturbed is most beneficial. Keeping your spine straight, begin chanting, starting with the "A," holding the "U" a little longer as it progresses through the chakras, and then ending on the "M" as the exhale of your breath ends. Chanting in a firm but not loud voice for at least 15 minutes is ideal if you genuinely want something substantial out of your meditative practice.

Regardless of technique, chanting Om is about connecting to the Divine. If your intention is sincere, everything else will fall into place. There are five things to know about visiting a Hindu temple.

To conclude this chapter, magic and meditation need to be discussed. Use the same altar as the first and add a yellow square in its center. Chant *Vayu Prithvi* four times twice a day until the candle burns out. This magic will make your Mind grounded, far more practical in your thinking, and

287

even more brilliant! You might take up singing or join a church choir to attune yourself to the heavenly and earthly vibrations of the universe – of 432 Hz.

Vayu Apas, or the Watery Part of Air

An orange field symbolizes this Tattva with a blue dot in its center and a white crescent moon in the center of that. In nature, it represents clouds. This Tattva is mysterious and unknown. It rules emotional speech and can come on heavy. The passions of Christ are akin to this Tattva with all its many stories with the twelve stations of the cross. The last supper and the crucifixion with Jesus rising from the dead to greet his twelve disciples are all under this Tattva of mysteries and the occult.

This Tattva is akin to all occult studies from Wicca to Mormonism, demonology, and Jehovah's Witnesses, the entire realms of psychic researchers and writings. All these occultism fields have answered regarding the unknown and mysterious.

Wicca (English: /ˈwɪkə/) is a modern Pagan religion. Religion scholars categorize it as a new religious movement and part of the occultist stream of Western esotericism. It was developed in England during the first half of the 20th century and was introduced to the public in 1954 by Gerald Gardner, a retired British civil servant.

Wicca draws upon a diverse set of ancient Pagan and 20th-century hermetic motifs for its theological structure and ritual practices. Wicca needed a central authority figure in those days. Its traditional core beliefs, principles, and practices were initially outlined in the 1940s and 1950s by Gardner and an early High Priestess, Doreen Valientes. The early practices were disseminated and published in books, and secretly written, and oral teachings were passed along to their initiates.

Wicca is typically duotheistic, worshipping and working with a Goddess and a God. These are traditionally viewed as the Triple Goddess and the Horned God. These deities may be regarded in a henotheistic way as having many different divine aspects, which can, in turn, be identified with many

290

diverse Pagan deities from other historical pantheons. For this reason, they are sometimes referred to as the "Great Goddess" and the "Great Horned God," with the adjective "great" connoting a deity that contains many other deities within their nature.

Some Wiccans refer to the goddess deity as the "Lady" and the god deity as the "Lord"; in this context, when "lord" and "lady" are used as adjectives, it is another way of referring to them as divine figures. These two deities are sometimes viewed as facets of a greater pantheistic divinity, which is regarded as an impersonal force or process rather than a personal deity. While duotheism or ditheism is traditional in Wicca, broader Wiccan beliefs range from polytheism to pantheism or monotheism, even Goddess monotheism. Others view them as the Universal God and Goddess Who proceed from the One.

291

Wiccan celebrations encompass the cycles of the Moon, known as sabots and commonly associated with the Goddess (female deity), and the processes of the Sun, seasonally based festivals known as Sabbats and widely associated with the Horned God (male Creator). An unattributed statement known as the Wiccan Rede is a popular expression of Wiccan morality, although Wiccans do not universally accept it. Wicca often involves the ritual practice of magic, though it is only sometimes necessary.

There are many variations in this core structure, and religion grows and evolves. It is divided into several diverse lineages, sects, and denominations, referred to as *traditions*, each with its organizational structure and level of centralization. Due to its decentralized nature, there is some disagreement over what constitutes Wicca. Some practices, collectively referred to as British Traditional Wicca (BTW), strictly follow the initiatory lineage of Gardner and consider the term *Wicca* to apply only to similar traditions but not to newer, diverse practices.

I was in two Wiccan groups that were very dangerous and unhealthy. The high priest of the Egyptian Lodge convinced himself that we were the Egyptian God – Osiris. I was also in a Minoan lodge that got involved in dangerous sex magic. Now, I practice my Wiccan as a solidarity in the Egyptian tradition.

The Book of Mormon: Another Testament of Jesus Christ - **Mormonism** is the religious tradition and theology of the Latter-Day Saint movement of restorationist of Christianity started by Joseph Smith in Western New York in the 1820s and 1830s. As a label, Mormonism has been applied to various aspects of the Latter-Day Saint movement, although there has been a recent push from the Church of Jesus Christ of Latter-day Saints (LDS Church) to distance themselves from this label. A historian, Sydney E. Ahlstrom, wrote in 1982, "One cannot even be sure whether [Mormonism] is a sect, a mystery cult, a new religion, a church, a people, a nation, or an American subculture; indeed, at different times and places, it is all of these." However, scholars and theologians within the Latter-Day Saint movement, including Smith, have often used "Mormonism" to describe the unique teachings and doctrines of the movement.

A prominent feature of Mormon theology is the Book of Mormon, which describes itself as a chronicle of early Indigenous peoples of the Americas and their dealings with God. Mormon theology includes mainstream Christian beliefs with modifications from belief in revelations to Smith and other religious leaders; this consists of the use of and faith in the Bible and other religious texts, including the Doctrine and Covenants and the Pearl of Great Price. Mormonism includes significant doctrines of eternal marriage, eternal progression,

294

baptism for the dead, polygamy or plural marriage, sexual purity, health (specified in the Word of Wisdom), fasting, and Sabbath observance.

The theology itself is not uniform; as early as 1831, and most significantly after Smith's death, various groups split from the Church of Christ that Smith established. Other than differences in leadership, these groups most significantly differ in their stances on polygamy, which the Utah-based LDS Church banned in 1890, and Trinitarians, which the LDS Church does not affirm.

The branch of theology which seeks to maintain the practice of polygamy is known as Mormon fundamentalism and includes several different churches. Other groups demonstrate Trinitarians, such as the Community of Christ (formerly the Reorganized Church of Jesus Christ of Latter-Day Saints) and describe their Doctrine as Trinitarian Christian restorationists. *Cultural Mormonism* is a term coined by cultural Mormons

295

who identify with the culture, mainly present in much of the American Southwest, but do not necessarily identify with the theology. The LDS church has billions of dollars in investment with very few charitable gifts it offers the needy.

What goes on in their temples has been influenced heavenly by the Freemans. Joseph Smith was a Freeman in his youth. In upstate New York, we are known for his abuse of psychedelic mushrooms. The format of his Book of Mormon was based on a novel with its famous passages, "and it came to pass".

At first, the Book of Mormon was just meant to be a novel, but Smith later cleverly turned the reader into a religious text. It was just the right time for our nation, right after the civil war, to believe in any form of promise or grace from the divine; this also was the same time when Armageddon doomsday-ers were preaching the end of the world and the coming of God's kingdom. Now, the only occultic religion preaching this, is the Jehovah's Witnesses.

The Mormon bishops are fired from their jobs because tithing falls very low. They lie about tithing being voluntary. I was harassed for me for not donating money when I spent a brief time with that occult. Anyway, the Book of Mormon reflected the widespread talk of those days and sum them all up, which was a key to its popularity.

Some say that the Book of Mormon borrowed a lot of mythologies from local Native American cultures. The religion likes to say that the natives of New York State were The Lenape, Mohicans, and Iroquois. These tribes were said to be light-skinned, with brown hair and hazel eyes. The Mormons preach that they were descendents of a lost Jewish tribe who left Israel thousands of years ago. The Mormons teach that the settlement was overrun by native tribes and the Jews who brought their tribes to life as they did. No DNA testing has proven this

297

fact. The Jews do not have recessive genes so as not to show up. Many local native stories have been adapted into the Book of Mormon.

The **Jehovah's Witness** member of a millennialism denomination developed within the more significant 19th-century Adventist movement in the United States. The faith has since spread worldwide. The Jehovah's Witnesses are an outgrowth of the International Bible Students Association, founded in 1872 in Pittsburgh by Charles Taze Russell. The Adventist movement emerged in the 1830s around the predictions of William Miller, who proclaimed that Jesus Christ would return in 1843 or 1844. When Christ did not return as Miller had prophesied, Adventists divided into several factions. During the 1870s, Charles Taze Russell established himself as independent and controversial.

Adventist teachers rejected the belief in hell as a place of eternal torment, and adopted a non-

Trinitarian theology that denied the divinity of Jesus; Also interpreted is the Second Coming following the literal translation of the original Greek term, *Parousia* ("presence"), suggesting that Christ would come as an invisible presence and that the Parousia, or "Millennial Dawn," already had occurred in 1874. The Coming of Christ's invisible presence signaled the end of the current order of society; it would be followed by his visible presence and the establishment of the millennial kingdom on Earth in 1914. Although the kingdom did not come, Russell's teachings motivated several volunteers to circulate his many books and pamphlets and a periodical, *The Watchtower*, and to recalculate the time of the Parousia.

In addition to the International Bible Students Association, Russell formed the Watch Tower Bible and Tract Society of Pennsylvania (1884) with himself as president. In 1909 he transferred the headquarters of the movement to Brooklyn.

299

Russell was succeeded as president in 1917 by Joseph Franklin Rutherford (Judge Rutherford; 1869–1942), who changed the group's name to Jehovah's Witnesses in 1931 to emphasize its members' belief that Jehovah, or Yahweh, is the true God and that the Witnesses were his specially chosen followers. Rutherford molded the Witnesses into a cadre of dedicated Evangelists, even equipping members with portable phonographs to play his "sermonettes" on street corners and in the living rooms of prospective converts. Under Rutherford's leadership, Russell's group became a tightly knit organization.

You might even say that the Tattva of the watery part of Air or Vayu Apas rules this book. If you were to practice magic or just meditation upon this Tattva, lay out on your altar an orange tablecloth and place a blue candle in glass on the altar. Draw a large blue dot with a white crescent mood in its center, chant Vayu Apas four times twice a day until the blue candle burns out. It is good to have its symbol and metaphors of life be brought to view to recall as pure impressions that are not to be interpreted at all.

This magic is good for understanding the mysteries in life and to feel the passion of the mysteries of God's love for you. Reading mysterious poetry like the I Ching or the Toa while doing this magic will help you gain a practical understanding it the text.

Reading the esoteric and mysterious saints of the Catholic Church under this Tattva influence will move you to a high level of enlightenment. Best of all, under this Tattva influences is your mysterious poetry about God and life that you can write yourself. Abstract art is yet one more expression of this Tattva. The artist channels deeply hidden abstract feelings though his/her Mind to the canvas. The more revolutionary – the more popular artist, I feel.

Anyway, I cared to mention those odd religious cults for you to understand that delusions can influence the Mind; and that it is far too common to think that our world religions are it canvas – deluded ways of thinking. Question: can we have clear thinking with this Tattva? Yes, we can, but do not try to understand these thoughts as they are metaphors of the truth and meant to ignite our curiosities only, with nothing factual about them. Understanding is like art; it makes a personal impression that differs from person to person.

Vayu Agni, or the
Fiery Part of Air

An orange field symbolizes Air with a large blue dot in its center with another item, a red upward triangle, this physical representation of nature of a warm sunny day. This Tattva is akin to philosophies of all kinds. Regarding philosophy, the first one in recorded history was Thales of Miletus (l. c. 585 BCE), traditionally regarded as the first Western philosopher and mathematician. He was born and lived in Miletus, a Greek colony on the west coast of present-day Turkey. He was referenced as the birthplace of Greek Philosophy because of his high standing as the First Philosopher, a title given to him by later Greek writers on the subject.

The philosopher Aristotle (384-322 BCE) was the first to call Thales the "First Philosopher", His claim was accepted because all his pronouncements were regularly regarded as accurate. None of Thales' works have survived -

what is known of his philosophy comes from fragments preserved in passages by later writers – but all agree that he pioneered the intellectual movement, which later would become known as Greek philosophy.

Aristotle is said to have accurately predicted the solar eclipse of 28 May 585 BCE and was a skilled astronomer, mathematician, statesman, engineer, and sage. Thales, it is said, was the first to ask the question, "What is the basic 'stuff' of the universe" and, according to Aristotle, claimed the First Cause was water because, among other attributes, water could change shape and move while remaining unchanging in substance.

Thales' inquiry into the nature of reality and its first causes should have posed created the world through supernatural means. However, there is no evidence that he was ever persccutcd for his work; on the contrary, he has been highly regarded.

The Socratic philosophers in ancient Greece were Socrates, Plato, and Aristotle. These are some of the most well-known of all Greek philosophers. In the tradition that Agni – Fire gives personal joy to each Tattva, what we are looking for in life, is the journey of a joyous way back to God. This goal will never be reached, so we enjoy the journey itself. Appreciating every moment in the journey is the journey's success.

Lao tzu or Laozi– Old Master. Philosophical Daoism – *the way* – traces its origins to Laozi, an extraordinary thinker who flourished during the sixth century B.C.E., according to Chinese sources. According to some modern scholars, however, Laozi is entirely legendary; there was never a historical Laozi. In religious Daoism, Laozi is revered as a supreme deity.

The name "Laozi" is best taken to mean "Old (*lao*) Master (*zi*)," and Laozi, the ancient philosopher, is said to have written a short book, which has come to be called simply the *Laozi*, after its putative author, a common practice in early China.

In the 82 sonnets of the Tao, we come to a sonnet stating that the Tao is ever too low to draw all waters and life to its basin; this meaning of low can be understood as evil too. In the Toa, bad and good are two sides of the same coin; to understand the Toa – God, you must realize wrong and good. Even the Lord Jesus Christ and Krishna evolved on the old planet Venus, where they were both very good and bad. They both came to our planet as ascended masters to help us all gain enlightenment; they had to understand both good and bad to function as a savior. Even we, as the people of today, must manifest righteous and evil lives to achieve our liberation for Maya and be enlightened; this is the Tao or the pathway back to our source.

Thoth (/θουθ, τουτ/; from Koinē Greek: Θώθ *Thóth*, borrowed from Coptic: Ⲑⲱⲟⲩⲧ *Thōout*,

Egyptian: *Ḏḥwtj*, the reflex of *ḏḥwtj*" [He] is like the Ibis") is an ancient Egyptian deity. In art, he was often depicted as a man with the head of an ibis or a baboon, animals sacred to him. His feminine counterpart was Seshat, and his wife was Ma'at. He was the God of the moon, wisdom, writing, hieroglyphs, science, magic, art, and judgment. His Greek equivalent is Hermes.

Thoth's chief temple was in the city of Hermopolis (Ancient Egyptian: *ḫmnw* /χaˈmaːnaw/, Egyptological pronunciation: "Khemenu," Coptic: Ϣⲙⲟⲩⲛ *Shmun*). Later known as *el-Ashmunein* in Egyptian Arabic, the Temple of Thoth was mostly destroyed before the beginning of the Christian era, but its very large pronaos still stood in 1826.

In Hermopolis, Thoth led "the Ogdoad," a pantheon of eight principal deities, and his spouse was Nehmetawy. He also had numerous shrines in other cities. Thoth played many vital and prominent roles in Egyptian mythology, such as maintaining

307

the universe and being one of the two deities (Ma'at) who stood on either side of Ra's solar baroque. In the later history of ancient Egypt, Thoth became heavily associated with the arbitration of religious disputes, the arts of magic, the system of writing, and the judgment of the dead.

Hermes Trismegistus (from Ancient Greek: Ἑρμῆς ὁ Τρισμέγιστος, "Hermes the Thrice-Greatest"; Classical Latin: *Mercurius ter Maximus*) is a legendary Hellenistic figure that originated as a syncretic combination of the Greek God Hermes and the Egyptian God Thoth. He is the purported author of Hermetical, a widely diverse series of ancient and medieval pseudo-epigraphical texts that lay the basis of various philosophical systems known as Hermeticism.

The wisdom attributed to this figure in antiquity, combined knowledge of the material and the spiritual world. The rendering of his writings attributed to him is relevant to those interested in the

308

interrelationship between the material and the divine. The figure of Hermes Trismegistus is found in Islamic and Bahá'í writings. In those traditions, Hermes Trismegistus was associated with the prophet Idris.

So, we can see that this early mathematician, doctor, and magician inspired the first worship of this new God, Tahuti. It wasn't until the Ptolemaic period that Tahuti was called Toth and associated with the Greek God Hermes. Some historians even say that he originates from The Egyptian delta. This new math is said to be used to build the Pyramids of Giza.

I have written earlier that personal Gods foster a lot of Mind noise; however, there are many threads of truth in all that chatting of the Mind, which is endless until otherwise simplified and settled. I have found the literary work of Confucius to be egotistical. The Tao and Hua Hu Ching are my select few who have clarity and logic to their text.

309

One thread of truth I'm aware of is that upon mankind gaining consciousness, our creator, Gods of the seventh Dimension, asked a league of his followers to honor and assist humanity. These followers refused and were asked to leave God's company. The reason those angels refused was jealousy because mankind is destined to grow beyond the level of those angels. How it stands now is that those fallen angels are not harmful, they have their agenda.

We also have our personal God's memories in our Minds. We all seem to have our personal God's guidance under the seventh-dimensional Godhead. Now, more nations are becoming atheistic, but are they a fact? Even atheists believe in superior power and divine intelligence at work in all creation. Our Godhead changes his ways of dealing with us with each astrological age. We have entered the age of Aquarius since the wars of independence under Napoleon Bonaparte, to the industrial revolution, free public education for all children, the atomic age, and the age of personal computers as we all currently have.

A form of worship called *Bhakti* devotion isn't asked of us nowadays. Education and mental prowess are in vogue today with the demonstrations of the personal wills of the freeman. Even on YouTube, anyone could be a star! They are even talking about the future stars of film and television being digital.

The reason why you might want to perform the Fiery part of Air Magic would be to get close to your spirit guides. They will assist you in your everyday tasks and with your highest ambitions.

To set up your altar, lay down an orange tablecloth with a blue candle. Draw on the glass a sizeable blue dot with a blue marker. Draw a red upward triangle in the center of the large blue dot. Chant *Vayu Agni* four times twice daily until the blue candle burns down. Good luck with a closer

311

relationship with your spirit guides. I love my guides!

Vayu Vayu, or the
Airy Part of Air

An orange field symbolizes the Airy part of Air with a large blue dot in the center with another blue dot in the center of that. In nature, it represents books of knowledge. The conflict between the divine and personal God has now sided with the personal God more than the divine. A strict adherence to dogmatic religions is represented in this Tattva.

The Vayu is the real, and this Tattva is the real to the real. There are only a few real laws of life in this Tattva – birth, eating and drinking, sleep, comfort, death, taxes, and sex. Most fittingly, this Tattva protects us from unnecessary Mind chatter about God and the meaning of life. In this Tattva, both God and life are fictional. The duality of this holding to a personal God and its release is taught in this airy part of Air. We are all grounded in the necessities of life here.

Yes, we have contradictions and conflicts in this one Tattva. The lessons are to accept your restrictions until you can grow out of them. You might be threatened with a judgment day of sorts. No worries – there is no such thing as death in any universe; we seem to have invented it to serve our third-dimensional Ego structure design. You see, the Ego is a designer and needs a clean canvas each time it paints a new piece of art – a life! Death is just the end of it, beginning with no knowledge of its course.

The *study of logic* is the Ego's last stronghold before its dissolution.

Logic: a science that deals with the principles and criteria of validity of inference and demonstration. The science of the formal principles of reasoning.

Reasoning is conducted or assessed according to strict principles of validity: "Experience is a better guide to this than deductive logic," Similar to science of reason, the science of deduction is the science of thought dialectics.

A system or set of principles underlying the arrangements of elements in a computer or electronic device to perform a specified task. The root noun to logic is logi in Greek or *the word* as in the OM - the first and only word that needs to be uttered. It is alpha and omega – the beginning and the end. All worlds apart from the Om are misleading and unnecessary. This OM lives in the first Dimension and is the root of all beings. It has two values: One and Zero. The logic of how it can hold two contradictive values is beyond human logic and rests with the divine.

In Astrology, there are two ways of using the Mind:

1. The Mercurial Way with its left-brained approaches to encounter differences.

2. The Neptunian Way with its right-brained approaches to encounter differences.

315

We have touched on this subject before, but only briefly. Mercury works with the physical brain, while Neptune works with the Mind. This Mind is eight-dimensional and non-physical. Its operations may be housed in part in the left hemisphere of the physical brain, but that is not where it operates. Our Minds are the seat of our consciousness which can even reach the thirteenth Dimension. Our consciousness lives beyond the duration of our human bodies.

In the thirteen Dimensions, it becomes immortal; this is a cointroduction but exists within the logic only God possesses; this act of charity forever creates a duality in life everywhere and has no beginning or end. We have always had our consciousness and always will. When we drop our consciousness in the thirteen Dimensions, we acquire a higher consciousness that still houses our lower consciousness.

Here in this Tattva is the conflict of spirit to the soul brought out in its fullest. The soul is just semi-divine, and the spirit has its infinite choices of growth and experiences. So, if they are both divine, where is the conflict? The conflict rests in the naïve nature of the soul with all its misunderstandings of life and God. The spirit has no misunderstandings as it realizes that it will never know God and lives free from that riddle. The soul, however, is caught up in this worthless riddle of life and God. We, as souls, are trapped in this endless quandary; this makes the soul semi-divine due to its foolishness.

Furthermore, the spirit is endless; it is divine. The soul is semi-divine and insane, which explains the insanity of life everywhere – it's all insanity! Mental illness is akin to this Tattva but in a healing way. The mentally ill all have unique insights into life that most do not have.

In the middle ages, royal courts had the mentally ill and deformed as good luck charms, and

317

the royals were fond of the simple advice given to them in the royal courts. God's court is the same way being us as His oddity. All else is sane in God's court but us. God blessed us as divine and accepted us being that way out of compassion. The peculiarity of who we are must serve God in some way. It opens the question to the question itself. Adding any reason or logic to it only sucks you into its chaos.

The reasons to perform the airy part of air magic could be to work you out of dogmatic religions to an absolute form of logic – or even the sense of the mind's undoing, as written in the Hua Hu Ching. I wrote the word Mind in lowercase to illustrate the lower Mind.

Set down an orange tablecloth with a blue candle in the glass to do this magic or meditation. Draw a large dark blue dot with a smaller lighter blue dot in the center. Chant *Vayu Vayu* four times twice a day until the candle burned down. Below are a few quotes from Lao Tso – Hua hu Ching

The Hua Hu Ching:

- "Kind prince; nothing in the realm of ideas is absolute; therefore, all efforts to form ideologies are ultimately futile."

- "Do exercise that develops your whole being and not just your body. Listen to music that bridges the three spheres of your being. Choose leaders for their virtue rather than their wealth or power. Serve others and cultivate yourself simultaneously. Understand that genuine growth comes from meeting and solving life problems in a way that harmonizes with yourself and others. You will be continually renewed if you follow these simple old ways."

- "Don't think you can attain total awareness and enlightenment without proper discipline and practice."

319

- "It is also a part of the cosmic law that what you say and do determines what happens in your life."

- "The Mind is just as immeasurable as the vast universe. An integral being settles his Mind just as the vast universe settles itself. He unites his Mind with the unnamable Subtle Origin of the multi-universe in which there is no past, present or future; This is how an integral being deals with his Mind."

- "To embrace all things also means that one rids oneself of any concept of separation; male and female, self and other, life and death.

- "Practicing kindness and selflessness, you naturally align your life with the Integral Way. Aligning your life with the Integral Way, you eliminate the illusory boundaries between people and societies, darkness and light, and life and death."

- "Any good person motivated to attain awareness of the truth should follow the Universal Way to calm his mind and harmonize it with all aspects of life."

- "Following the Universal Way means practicing selflessness and unconditionally extending virtue to the world. In this way, one not only eliminates the heavy contamination accumulated throughout many lifetimes but may also bring about the possibility of restoring one's original divine nature and becoming an integral being of the multi-universe."

- "Most of the world's religions serve to strengthen attachments to false concepts such as self and other, life and death, heaven and earth, and so on."

- "Dualistic thinking is a sickness. Religion is a distortion. Materialism is cruel. Blind spirituality is unreal. Chanting is no more holy than listening to the murmur of a stream, counting prayer beads no more sacred than simply breathing, and religious robes no more spiritual than work clothes. Don't get caught up in spiritual superficialities if you wish to attain oneness with the Tao. Instead, live a quiet, simple life free of ideas and concepts. Find contentment in the practice of undiscriminating virtue, the only true power. Your virtue will become a sanctuary for yourself and all beings giving to others selflessly and anonymously, radiating light throughout the world and illuminating your darkness. This fact is what is meant by embodying the Tao."

If you should perform this type of magic, you might be more telepathic. You could get your messages across to others directly. You could be able to read others' minds as well. You might even be able to pick up messages from God, who watches over you for better guidance. Also, your intellect is better. Your thoughts will be faster and more precise.

Vayu Akasha or the Airy part of Aether

This Tattva is represented by an orange open field with a blue dot in it middle with a purple or black egg in the middle of that. In nature its image is the truth. The fact that it has no visible image is apparent. The truth cannot be represented in nature apart from nature being truth itself.

Being that we are in a realm of duality, this makes the truth personal to the individual. Nowhere in nature can we find the truth to satisfy all. Apart from that, nature is seen as true here with its laws of physics as seen in nature and man. However, the laws of physics vary from multiverse to multiverse which makes them arbitrary and nonsensical. As you can see, in this Tattva, all is seen as relative. There is no real overall truth that vast all multiverses, Dimensions and more.

You might wonder, well, what must we do then? The answer is to live along with nature. We chose to be here, so simply finding out why you chose to be here is all that we can do. In truth, doing otherwise will only fill your head with too many abstract concepts if you were to find out. At the least, why we chose to be here in the first place is the question. So, what must we do then? Simply just be you is all you can do and face each issue in your life one at a time.

What is essential about this Tattva is the cleaning of the Mind and brain- or to say higher and lower Mind. Zazen meditations are the cleaning of my soul. To practice this meditation, you sit on the floor in a chair with either your eyes open or closed. You try to think about nothing at all. You dismiss any thought that comes into your head. What you want to experience is the peace that this meditation brings you alone; this peace cannot be described in words as words with only destroy such peace and mislead you to delusions; this peace is to be carried with you in your conscious hours during the day and

325

at night. People will feel your inner peace and love you for it. The lower Mind does not need to be focused on anything to do this meditation well. You just allow this peace to overtake you.

This shall be the briefest chapter in this book as not too much can be written about its nature as it is nonverbal. If you were to perform its magic, you would know how it is important to deal with things in your life now. Perhaps you might not even know what is important or not? This magic is done like the other magic in the Vayu series, but you place a purple egg in the center of the blue dot and chant *Vayu Akasha* four times twice a day until the candle burns out. If done right, you will find the silence in between the works or noises in your day where the peace of God can be experienced.

Akasha- Aether

The Aether, or a White Field with a Black Teardrop Egg

This book's following five chapters are non-physical and possess no tangible properties. Poetry and mythology are the only two means of explaining their realities, as words alone cannot serve. The symbol for this Tattva is a white field with a black teardrop egg in its center. Duality is represented here with its black and white at opposite poles. Vayu's duality only worsens here as there is not one thing that they both have in common. Life and God were common and recurring within the Vayu Tattva, but there are no commonalities in this Tattva. It's all binary as in - on and off, yes and no, stop and go.

In the Greek astrological mythology of Castor and Pollux, Castor was the mortal son of King Tyndareus, while Pollux was the immortal son of Zeus. Pollux always knew of his immortality, but

Castor always tried to obtain it. The truth is that both are immortal, but Castor never fully realizes is like his brother Pollux. According to the myth of the two brothers, the constellation of Gemini is depicted as two twins: Castor and Pollux.

Castor and Pollux, identical twins, were inseparable in their looks and actions. Castor was a great horseman, and Pollux was a great fighter. Together, they went with Jason on the Argo and saved the ship from a terrible storm. When Castor was killed in battle, Pollux pleaded with Zeus to bring him back. Zeus agreed to immortalize Castor and Pollux if they spent half their time on the Earth and the other half on Mount Olympus. Since then, when sailors saw the constellation of Gemini, they would know their journey would bring good luck.

However, seeing only one star foretells terrible luck. Like the two brothers who have one thing in question - of his immortality, so are we. In our third Dimension, we create birth, life, and death for the sake of the art; this art is on a grand level beyond our mortal Mind's comprehension. Art, as we know it, is a left-brained malfunction. The art of the third Dimension is right-brained. We need an old-world faith in the continuum of life. My hypothesis is: *As you think, you always believe and always will be.*

The very act of thinking is divinity itself. The Latin cogito, ergo sum, is usually translated into English as "*I think*; therefore, *I am*," is the "first principle" of René Descartes' philosophy. The logic of the above hypothesis can be explained as while we, thus, reject all of which, we can entertain the slightest doubt and even imagine that it is false.

We quickly suppose that there is neither God, nor sky, nor bodies and that we have neither hands nor feet nor, finally, a body, but we cannot, in the same way, suppose that we are not while we are in doubt of the truth of these things; for there is an aversion in conceiving that what one thinks does not

330

exist at the very time when it is thought of is believed to be often thought of.

René Descartes (31 March 1596- 11 February 1650) was a famous French philosopher and physicist. He wrote essential books in math, physics, and especially philosophy. His dualism statement *combined soul, Mind, and body* theories and elements into one concept: *a dualistic view of Mind and matter.* What Descartes was touching on in this dualistic theory of Mind and matter is an eight-Dimension value of – power discernment! (The Lord Krishna Apara Brahman - form) rules over the eight-Dimension as (Para Brahman – formless) rules over the ninth. However, both are the aum. The realm of Lord Krishna is the highest we can go to with our human Minds; however, with the AUM or Om, we can go higher to the super spirit realms to the thirteenth Dimension. We have multiple spirits in the eighth Dimension but just one in the ninth. The Ninth Dimension is where our

331

sanity is restored. Even the logic of Krishna is insane but blessed us anyway to help us grow. Is Krishna one God? No, he is many! With many of his truths making this truth even for ridiculous thought, it is still blessed to help us grow; this blessing understands the ridiculous riddle of God and life, and can work with it. Krishna has 108 names, but there are just five for you.

1.   Rishikesh – Lord of all the senses.
2.   Keshava – The one who has long black matted hair.
3.   Murlimanohar – He looks beautiful with a flute.
4.   Ranchod – The one who runs away from the battlefield.
5.   Gopala – Cowherd.
6.   Dwarkadhish – The lord of Dwarka.
7.   Nandakumar – The son of Nanda.

Each of the 108 names takes on the blessing in its way. We need a finite number of which we need to reach our left-brained reasoning, which is limited. To create what is simultaneously divine and finite is ridiculous; however, with the Mind of God, all things are made possible.

I again mention this *old-world faith* in what God can do; this *old-world faith* corrected the mistake of our separation from our source in the split second it occurred. However, this split second needed to be faster as it created many dreamlike realms beyond number. He felt that we had to go to them to understand how wrong it was, but in the act of this understanding, we are here in our separation currently.

The fact remains that it is not worth trying to understand an already bad idea. We love God so much that we had to understand what happened so it would not happen again. We had these separations an uncountable number of times and avowed to get it right this one and one last time, but we always need to keep the peace. God has an understanding laugh over it all.

If you want to understand the split further, buy my second book – Personal growth in the multi-dimensional Multiverse. Balboa Press 2021 Frank Marcello Antonetti.

You might want to practice magic or meditation upon this Tattva – Akasha. The reasons you might be to understand your true immortality! You might want to understand that death is an illusion we created to grasp a higher meaning of the art of the third Dimension. You might want to understand modern art as a means of personal and emotional growth as well as mental progressions to gain a glimpse of your immortality. You can study contemporary art and understand life – they go hand in hand. As we progress as a race, we will realize this very fact.

To set your altar, lay a white cloth with a black candle in glass. Draw a dark gray teardrop egg

334

with a dark gray marker on the glass. Chant *Akasha* four times with an Om twice a day until the candle burns out. If this magic is done right, spirit will touch and illuminate you to an all-new world or abstract concept of life. Try to avoid making sense of these concepts, that will only mislead you. The left brain cannot analyze such experiences that pure spirit can endow upon you. Art is the best way that I can write a tangible expression of it, but there might be others too.

Suppose you can study modern art, from Impressionism to the Cubic period. What are the three characteristics of modern art? While contemporary modern art can be hard to define, some essential features are commonly associated with it. Contemporary modern art is often abstract, experimental, and process based. The modern art movement has nine periods - The most influential (1) Impressionism; (2) Fauvism; (3) Cubism; (4) Futurism; (5) Expressionism; (6) Dada; (7)

335

Surrealism; (8) Abstract Expressionism; and (9) Pop Art.

Try studying each period on Youtube and Google will get you a start. I do it occasionally to deepen my understanding of the various art forms. I would also study each artist with the times they lived in with the current art movement to their days. See what they had donated to each movement and why? Modern had an eye on the future, so they say. Start your education today! - an education that will help you grow.

So, does art have anything to do with binary functioning? Well, all the colors of paint mixed together makes black paint, while all the colors of light focused on the same point creates white light. In this manner, they are the same.

Akasha Prithvi, or the Earthly part of the Aether

This Tattva symbol is a white field and a black teardrop in its center with a yellow square in the center of that drop. The subconscious Mind is created here and works biliary with both hemispheres of our brains – left and right to make thoughts. Prithvi is the grounding of Akasha, and the ground is our subconscious minds. Akasha is the divine, so too are our subconscious Minds. Our subconscious Mind can conceive of infinity, but not even our right brain can. Our subconscious Mind can conceive of infinity, which our right brain cannot do. Also, our subconscious minds have a glimpse into the divinity of God, but they cannot prove it due. One clue I can give you about the logic of God is that it is all open-minded. A thread of truth between them all is the logic of God in common. God is as high as He is low, etc. – Lao Tso in the Hua Hu Ching.

337

I want to explain why our subconscious Minds are divine now. It is divine in its ways of finding connections and commonalities between opposites. Many people want to say that it's a storehouse of pains and inflictions that are meant to protect you. That is true as well, but only on a superficial basis. The subconscious Mind is 90% of our functioning brains. We only have a simple idea of its nature.

The shadow is the storehouse of inflictions and operates on our animus and anima. We feel we killed God to gain consciousness, and God will attach us. The thirteenth Dimension is the life and death of our consciousness. When our consciousness dies, we become the drop that becomes the ocean of life. The hypothesis is that: *if it happened, it would always happen.* So, both are valid in the mysteries of that divine Dimension. We have united with all and are separate at the same time.

As we understand our subconscious Mind, more of the mysteries of God and life will be revealed. We will learn how to program our subconscious Minds in a way that can serve us; it will be the basis of our supercomputer. The atomic bomb could only have had its math logic worked out with a physical computer. Now, when computing makes use of our subconscious minds it will outdo any physical computers that man can make.

When this shadow touches the animus, we feel a misdirected anger from God, authorities, or men. Many criminals have this influencing them.

When the shadow touches the Anima, love relationships to have might be challenging and always with a price. There also may be an evil woman. Many rapists and child abusers are influenced in this way.

I have a shadow anima with a mother who throws away my teddy bears as a child, evil schoolgirls, a green card marriage that put me in jail

339

for 15 days, and shallow troublesome lady friends. All of this is a result of my shadow touching my Anima. I was not very close to my father as to have gotten overly involved with him, so there was no animus problem with me, but I never really liked him, I can admit. Both examples are at the very top of the subconscious Mind. However, the real Mind is much lower than that. We have yet to be awakened to it. Can you imagine time traveling twenty thousand years in the future and trying to relate to humanity? It would be impossible. First, they would be speaking telepathically, and second, they would fully use their Minds. We would be seen as fearful wild savages who cannot relate to anything.

So, what else can we say about the earthly part of Aether?

Our intuitive inspirations are one.

Our rejection of delusions is another.

340

I say intuitive because they come from our right brain and, in part, our subconscious Mind. You see here that Akasha is not pure when touching upon the lower four elements, so this inspiration is personal. Only when we talk about the airy part of Aether and higher do we gain true messages from the divine.

Our rejection of delusions is helpful to live on Earth. Many false ideas are fed into our Minds daily. Without such a function, life would be full of diseases and mental illnesses. The lords of the air are both demonic and divine simultaneously. They walk the middle path elegantly. Yes, they start wars and diseases to plague humanity, but not without permission from Shamballa's great and high lord. Sanat Kumara permitted both covid and the war in Ukraine.

Covid virus explorations were a joint venture of the Americans and Chinese. However, the Chinese are lying about their low covid deaths.

Consequently, it will get a lot worse before it gets better. The Chinese covid vaccine is ineffective. The United States of America has two of the most effective vaccines available. The war in Ukraine will cause the end of the Russian Federation and a rebirth of a western modeled Russian nation. Russia has a very high poverty rate with a poor standard of living. All of that will improve in due time. Covid had to happen to unite the world under its banner. Unfortunately for the American people, it was the short-sightedness of then-President Trump, in not closing our border early on at the first signs of covid to save American lives.

Still, it is odd that our great lord in Shamballa would work alongside the lords of the air. However, they need to as a grounding for even finer growths to come. The nation of Israel would have never been established without the Holocaust. Even the black plague in medieval Europe had excellent growth after one-third of its people had passed on.

Dr. Edward Jenner created the world's first successful vaccine. He found out that people infected with cowpox were immune to smallpox. In May 1796, English physician Edward Jenner expanded on this discovery and inoculated 8-year-old James Phipps with matter collected from a cowpox sore on the hand of a milkmaid. Smallpox disease was its first test and proved to be a success for vaccinations in general for all times to come. The problem was that the vaccination was overlooked for a long time until it was used. The covid vaccine and its many boosters have saved countless lives so far.

I mentioned earlier that this Tattva could clear away delusions. Yes, it can be like a doctor from a very high alien culture coming here to help us. Poverty and poor health are delusions we can clear up using this Tattva. The problem is that many have blocks due to the inflictions of the anima or animus. Our subconscious Mind is neutral to anything good or bad. Sigmund Freud was wrong in his depictions of the subconscious.

Now, the subconscious Mind can block past lives out so we can focus on our current life; this is for our benefit, but we need to understand why. Many people have been healed by finding past life knowledge. There also is a lot of past life knowledge that has nothing to do this our current life. I even believe in parallel lives, as I mentioned earlier. These are what I call – coauthor lives. In these lives, many souls claim to have been Cleopatra in a past life. The truth is, only in a passive–coauthor form, but not in an active state as Cleopatra's main soul-driven force, which was just one soul. I believe that very highly developed aliens live in this world that care for us and help us in times of need. We have many over-souls who are projections of who we are but in a more expanded form.

You should open yourselves up to higher love to heal these blockages. Try magic or meditation on this Tattva. To perform this magic, lay out a white cloth and put the same candle down, but this time adds a yellow square in the center of the teardrop. Chant *Akasha Prithvi* four times a day, twice a day, until the candle burns out. Think about opening your Mind and heart to a higher form of love and let it all in. If you can do this magic right, your subconscious Mind will open to you its secrets – many past lives may submerge to the surface.

Akasha Apas, or the Watery part of Aether

The watery part of Aether symbol is a white field with a black teardrop in its center with a white crescent moon in the center of that inner symbol. Its physical symbol is the human heart. This Tattva works through our hearts to open us up to the healing of the separation from our source. Honestly, this is the definition of love – the reunification with God. The heart's key on the piano is naturally F, and for its healing F#. You may benefit from listening to songs in F# or playing their music on the piano. The key signature does have six sharps to deal with – Only F is natural in that key. However, F# minor only has three sharps to deal with and is lighter key but not with the same intensity.

The color of the heart chakra is green. Green is a balancing hue ruled by the sign Libra – law. Yes, there are laws of the heart, as in fidelity to marriage. I have heard of women who divorced their husbands just for cheating once. A woman demands exclusive devotion. Females from Columbia do not go out with their lady friends much; they are always seen with their husbands. Columbians take relationships to an all-new level of seriousness. The law of the heart is called – reflectivity; do to others as you wish to be done to you – the golden rule by Jesus Christ; this is the sum of all Jewish laws of old – and to me, the only law that makes sense.

Why does traditional relationship demand so many exclusives? I do not know. When Israel was a young nation- it had Kibbutz. In a conventional Kibbutz, the group raises the children, not the parents alone. In a Kibbutz, they do not have traditional marriages – they are all single and have sex with whomever they please. I feel that this is a very advanced system – even for humanity! Today, there are over 270 kibbutzim in Israel. They have significantly diversified since their agricultural beginnings; many are privately managed.

347

Regardless of their status, the Kibbutz offers a unique insight into Israeli society.

Additionally, they are fascinating places to visit. I do not know that the Kibbutz discourages marriage and being distant from their children today; it depends on the Kibbutz. Moreover, This Kibbutz arrangement will serve as a world model one day. The Kibbutz of old used to be agricultural, but today, information technology rules with some manufacturing as well.

When the crescent moon touches this Tattva, we feel emotionally aetheric. Things go our way because we are more in touch with the divine, and surrender to its power. We can empathize more with others under this influence; this is a beautiful excuse to practice the magic for this Tattva. You will get more in touch with others and your spirit guides to help you. Your heart will feel the love of the universe. The universe wants you to manifest God

348

as a God in your own right. Growth is the way that our universal Logi will help us.

Regarding logis, we have planetary logis, Solar logi, Galactic logis, and Universal logi. We even have multi-dimensional logi counsels to rule over countless universes in a particular dimension.

The influence of this Tattva will teach you of universal love – all souls could *be a God* in this universe. With this universal love, you cheer them all on to their success. Your heart is open to the growth of other people. The idea is that we all will be 'God made manifest' together – not one being left behind! We feel the success in sharing this love with all life forms of any status of life currently. We honor all living life forms as God. The eating of meat is against universal love. If you must eat meat, keep it minimal.

The Indian nation is close to this universal love. When the British entered India at the Battle of

349

Plassey on 23 June 1757, the government only then started to change their diets to eat meat.

However, Archaeological evidence from the 5,000-year-old Harappan civilization in India shows that a wide variety of animals were consumed. Moreover, animal sacrifice was considered an essential part of the Vedic culture 3,000 years ago. So when did India become vegetarian? After the fourth century BC, vegetarianism began gaining respect in India, particularly among Buddhists, Jains, and Hindus. But most Hindus continued to the Rig Veda period (c. 1500 BC) by not eating cow meat.

After the fourth century, meat was popularly consumed by the lower classes, called "the untouchables". These untouchables were the lowest class of people in the Indian hierarchy of social order. The upper classes and religious population remained vegetarians to set the standard in India. Yes, they did have animal sacrifices, but only the poor lower classes eats the meat provided for them by the various temples.

When angry or frightened, people find it hard to open to this Tattva. We will have times in our lives when this doorway will be closed. We are only hurting ourselves by letting this Tattva doorway remain closed. We may feel inflicted and unforgiving to abuse others who may be trying to love us. This victim's attitude must be healed, even if it takes many lifetimes to repeat the injury to heal it. There will be helpers on your path of healing; what it takes is a little willingness and openness to see things differently.

I know of two men thrown around as an infant to toughen them up by their fathers. Their fathers taught them to be too feminine and gentle. I was a little like that, but I fought my father back with my protests. Due to my autism, I do not always defend myself, even now. My duty in life is to use my self-love, and I must be understood by others to teach them to treat me respectably. However, proper behavior makes it far from easy to get along with others. I was told, in business, that a professional demeanor protects one. Anyway, those two victims grew up to be the type that control others with their anger. These types only have a shallow feeling toward others. Infancy traumas are almost impossible to get over; they usually take their offense out on the closest people to them, this is called transference. This transference is very immature and irresponsible. Those types typically do not turn out well as adults.

To heal this trauma, one must be mature and responsible for their behavior and aware of how one treats others to allow the healing to enter. Forgiveness is the key here. True forgiveness is when the original issue is no longer affecting you. It is not with a word saying – I'm sorry. You can be hiding grievances behind your words. Try to give this magic a chance.

352

Set out a white tablecloth with a black candle to do this magic. Take a black marker and draw a teardrop egg with a white crescent moon in its middle. Chant *Akasha Apas* four times, twice a day until the candle burns down. Meditate over its symbol with the candle to help it along. Wear green clothing, if possible, to balance your heart chakra, to allow the Tattva energies to come in better.

My closing words about this Tattva are that, it is one of my favorites. Reading this book, you will come across your favorite Tattva. There will be some magic that works and others that will not work for you. Our characters have a lot to do with them all. It is best to find the Tattva that works best, and to overlook the rest until the time in your life when its doorway has opened for it.

I wish you the best of luck with this very special Tattva. I know that this Tattva will bring blessings from the universe into your heart. From

353

your heart, it will radiate to your whole body and soul.

Now, to perform such magic/mediations using this Tattva, you set up your altar like the others, but on the candle, glass draw a silver crescent moon in the middle of the black egg. Chant *Akasha Apas* four times, twice a day until the candle burns out. You will open your heart to God's compassion, and you will be able to heal past traumas.

Akasha Agni, or the
Fiery part Aether

The fiery part of the Aether symbol is a white field with a black teardrop egg in its center, with an upward red triangle in the center of that. Practicing Kundalini Yoga can be used as a tool to expand consciousness and reach a state of enlightenment, joy, and boundless love. The term *Shakti* refers to multiple ideas. Its general definition is the dynamic energy responsible for the universe's creation, maintenance, and destruction.

It is identified as female energy because Shakti is responsible for the creation, as mothers are responsible for birth. The Pingala nadi, an origin point of pranic energy, travels the length of the spinal cord, weaving in and out of the seven chakras. From Sanskrit, Pingala means "tawny – orange, brown," and nadi means "channel" or "flow." Pingala nadi is also called the Surya, or sun, nadi because it is related to *solar energy*. Ida is associated with lunar energy. The word ida means "comfort" in Sanskrit. Idā has a *moonlike* nature and feminine energy with a cooling effect. The (sushumna nadi – a joyful mind) connects the first muladhara Chakra to the seventh Sahasrara chakra and is the path for the ascent of kundalini energy, from the base of the spine to the crown of the head. It is considered the central channel for the flow of prana throughout the body. When the Ida and Pingala nadi are channeled into the Sushumma nadi, you obtain universal balance and experience an unknown order. You will be at peace with yourself and all in creation.

    •   The *Sacral Chakra* is the seat of our soul and not our lower spirit, which is the heart chakra. Our upper spirit's home is our Crown Chakra. We face death here and see it as a delusion. We socialize here with two others and work out sexual and emotional needs for companionship.

- The *Throat Chakra* is where we sing the songs of divinity. Singing can also be speaking! Healing words from the divine are channeled through this Chakra. We have a charismatic effect on others using this Chakra. Speaking convincingly and boldly are signs of a healthy throat Chakra when aligned with the Solar plexus and Sacral Chakras. Communications, in general, are of this Chakra – speech, healing works, prayer, writing, and singing. We unite with the divine through prayer!

- The *Crown Chakra*. This Chakra was one thousand pedals and is where they connect to all spirits. This Chakra is ninth dimensional. All spiritual beings are in harmony with this Chakra. We even have a direct link with God through the infinite spirit sons of God to us, individually. Our whole life course and destiny can be changed if we open to our Crown Chakra. Original thought is rare, but those who are convinced they have original thought can create universes by that lie. More

357

universes are created employing this lie than grains of sand at your favorite beach. We try to get an understanding of God by manifesting Him as much as possible; this is a false idea. No matter how hard you try, it's impossible to understand God. He is the greatest unknowable. What God can tell you won't be in words but a reassurance that all is just fine as they are at rest in that peace.

• Chakra of the beyond. Some say we have 144,000 Chakras, with only twelve associated with the human body. I just mentioned the seven Hindu traditional Chakra, but there are five more – One down by our feet and four over our heads, all in Aetheric space. These 144,000 are divided into groups of twelve, with the seven I mentioned.

Apart from Hindu understandings, the fiery part of Akasha is where we gain vision into Akasha – The Spirit – Aether. First, the spirit is on a higher plane of vibration than where we are currently. What one gets out of these two isn't the product, but

358

the inner peace you have experienced in the journey to reach that goal, for e.g. art or music, etc.

First, get your white table covering your altar and place a black candle upon it to do this magic. On the glass of the candle, draw in black ink the tear drop egg with an upward red triangle in its center. Chant *Akasha Agni* four times twice a day until the candle burns down.

If you can remember just one thing – We are all One!

Akasha Vayu, or the
Airy part of Aether

This Tattva symbolizes a white field with a black egg in its center and a light blue dot in the middle of that egg shape. Its representation in Nature is not seen but experienced as one's intuition – Extrasensory perception, or ESP. In this chapter, I will write about various forms of divine knowledge unknown to most that I gathered from many esoteric sources and my own automatically inspired writings, as seen below.

I truly believe that the human intuition is of our divine Minds and not of our lower brains. What we deem as new insights are gathered from your Mind reaching higher realms to inform you on certain matters of life. Have you ever had an insight that proved to be valid over time that just came into your Mind to your lower brain like a light flashing? Yes, it's only human to experience such a phenomenon.

Our personal gods of the seventh Dimension used our intuition to guide us. One odd thing about reality is – God isn't aware that we are here in Maya in the separation for His graces. He recognizes us to be right at His right-hand side by Him. God can only see His aspects of Himself- His infinite Sons as Gods themselves as He is. There is just one thing that makes us different from God; and that is we, as His sons, want to know who God is. God is the great unknowable, though. The thread of truth in these two statements is that God uses His infinite eternal Sons to understand Himself. The truth is that this is the meaning of all Life everywhere. If not for this yearning to know – no life anywhere could be possible.

The reason why God doesn't know Himself is the reason why He exists – it is the yearning to know and grow. God grows though His infinite, eternal Son. God is seen in math as the negative zero.

For God to exist He must not exist; for God to know who He is, he must be empty of all ideas of who He is – it is our job to achieve such knowledge, not God's. That is why we exist. We will never know who God is, as that would be the end of all life everywhere. Another thing that separates us from God is that God doesn't question who He is – we do. God is whole and complete in His unknown, mysterious Nature that we will never understand.

The airy part of the Aether symbol is a white field with a black teardrop egg in its center and a blue ball in the center. It has no physical representation, but it uses intuition. The Mind is not the brain with its two hemispheres of the Cerebral cortex, midbrain, and Cerebellum. The human and animal brains all have their many parts. The Mind is beyond the fleshly brain and reaches through many Dimensions until the last one – the eighth Dimension. Psychologists for many years have tried and failed to understand what the Mind is. We believe it may use the fleshly brain, but it is beyond that. The Mind relates to its two other partners – the Heart and Chakra systems. Mind matters in both the Heart and the 144,000 Chakra associated with our brains - Mind. So, we all have three Minds that work as One Mind! We call this one Mind - the Mind! The Chakra's Mind is our consciousness; our heart's Mind is our emotions; our brain's Mind is our knowingness of matters. I will delineate all three Minds now:

The Three Minds of our Mind

- _Our Fleshly Brain Mind_ is our sense of all-knowingness. We know all our past lives in this Mind but are not close to them to create a focus for the life we are in currently. It would take time and patience to recover those lives, though it might prove impractical or useless. I have discovered that past lives do not help me much in knowing them. I had a parallel life that explains a lot of my fortune from my army and the government pays I get currently. The hypothalamus, pituitary gland, and pineal gland serve as orchestra conductors that signal the other glands in the body to emit hormones to perform their functions. Eastern Gurus mistook the Pineal gland as the third eye and omitted where the crown Chakra might be. The third eye has no physical ground in the body like any other of the Chakras do not.

- *The Intellect of the Heart.* The Heart is yet another aspect of the Mind. The Heart offers an emotional feel to matters. Our divine spirits use this Intellect of the Heart to keep incarnated (Jivi – one who incarnates) on the right path. The Heart is used to keep the soul in a more spirited orientation. Without the Heart's intellect, the soul might go astray. We have an empathetic feel to life through this intellect. You might think the soul is in charge, but it follows directly from the Heart. Some are heartless, though. These types have a victim mentality and do not trust in love. They have separated themselves from their divine spirits and are astray.

- _The Chakra System._ The Chakra System is yet another aspect of the Mind we must consider. All 144,000 Chakras are at work to hold this energy field called the Mind together. The Mind may use the brain and Heart, but it houses among the 144,000 Chakra in Aetheric space around our body. We, as humans, use mostly the primary seven Chakras with their associated others. We need to grow into our higher Chakra. The third root race, the Lemurian, lived in Lemuria. This race redated our current Arian race by 35 million years. Why did they live in the lower astral plane? They were over 10 feet tall with very tall heads. Their heads houses the remaining four Chakras on their feet. They had a universal awareness too. They lived in a peacefully organized society.

Since the Mind has been explained, we can talk about the direct influence Akasha may have as it is acting air-like. What happens is called – trends, periods or growth, epics in history, and last phases of human growth.

I will explain the four areas of growth trends now.

The Four Trends:

1. *Phases in human growth are* according to Theosophy – the literary works of H.P Blavatsky- Human life has had many phases of development in what she termed Root Races. **Root races** are stages in human evolution in the esoteric cosmology of theosophist Helena Petrovna Blavatsky, as described in her book *The Secret Doctrine* (1888). These races existed mainly on now-lost continents. Blavatsky's model was developed by later

theosophists, most notably William Scott-Elliot in *The Story of Atlantis* (1896) and *The Lost Lemuria* (1904). Annie Besant further developed the model in *Man: Whence, How and Whither* (1913). Besant and Scott-Elliot relied on information from Charles Webster Leadbeater obtained by "astral clairvoyance." Rudolf Steiner elaborated in his writing about Atlantis *and Lemuria* in 1904. Rudolf Steiner, and subsequent theosophist authors, have called the periods associated with these races **Epochs;** the author Steiner felt that the term "race" was not adequate anymore for modern humanity).

The *first root race* was "ethereal," i.e., they were composed of aetheric matter. They reproduced by dividing like an amoeba. Earth was still cooling at that time. Mount Meru was the first mountain to rise out of the stormy primeval ocean.

The *second root race* lived in Hyperborea. The second root race was colored golden yellow.

367

Hyperborea included what is now Northern Canada, Greenland, Iceland, Scandinavia, Northern Asia, and Kamchatka. The climate was tropical because Earth had not yet developed an axial tilt. The esoteric name of their continent is *Plaksha*; they called themselves the *Kimpurshas*, and they reproduced by budding.

The <u>*third root*</u> race, the Lemurian, lived in Lemuria. The esoteric name of Lemuria is *Shalmali*. Lemuria, according to Theosophists, existed in a large part of what is now the Indian Ocean, including Australia; and its last remnants still extend into the South Pacific Ocean, the Australian continent, the island of New Guinea, and the island of Madagascar. Lemuria sank gradually and was eventually destroyed by incessantly erupting volcanoes. In the late 19th and early 20th centuries, it was thought by geologists that the age of the Earth was only about 200 million years (Because radioactive dating had not yet come into use), so the

368

geological epochs were believed to have occurred at a much later time than is thought to be the case today.

According to traditional Theosophy, the Lemurian root race began 34½ million years ago in the middle of what was then believed to be the Jurassic, but were astral in their Nature and world. The Lemurian race was much taller and more significant than our current race—the first three subraces of the Lemurians reproduced by laying eggs. Still, the fourth subrace, beginning sixteen and a half million years ago, began to reproduce like modern humans.

As Lemuria was slowly submerged due to volcanic eruptions, the Lemurians colonized the areas surrounding Lemuria, namely Africa, Southern India, and the East Indies. The descendants of the Lemurian root race, according to traditional Theosophy, include the Capoid race, the

Congoid race, the Dravidians, and the Australoid race.

According to Theosophy, the _fourth root race_, the Atlantean, arose approximately 4,500,000 years ago in Africa from the fourth subrace of the Lemurians in a part of Africa that that subrace had colonized in the area now inhabited by the Ashanti. According to Theosophists, the first Atlantean subrace resulted from the last or seventh Lemurian subrace, Chan Shusha Manu, which migrated first to the south of the Atlantean continent, and from there they migrated further north. The esoteric name of Atlantis is _Kusha_. The Atlantean root race had Mongolian features; they began with bronze skin and gradually evolved into the red American Indian, brown Malayan, and yellow Mongolian races because some Atlanteans eventually migrated to the Americas and Asia. The seven subraces of the Atlantean root race were:

1. The Ramoahal

2. The Tlavati (Cro-Magnons)

3. The Toltec (a term that Theosophists use as a synonym for the Atlantean ancestors of the American Indians)

4. The Turanian

5. The Original Semites (i.e., Phoenicians)

6. The Akkadians, and

7. The Mongolians migrated to and colonized Central Asia, East Asia, and Southeast Asia.

The descendants of the Atlanteans, according to traditional Theosophy, include those of the Mongolian race, the Malayan race, and the American Indian race, as well as some people of what in the late 19th and early 20th centuries was called the "olive-skinned" Mediterranean race.

According to Powell, during the long period when Atlantis was ruled by the Toltecs (the ancestors of the Amerindians), the civilization of Atlantis was at its height; This was the period

371

between about 1,000,000 and 900,000 years ago, called the *Golden Age of Atlantis*. The Atlanteans had many luxuries and conveniences.

Their capital city was called *The City of the Golden Gates*. At its height, it had two million inhabitants. There were extensive aqueducts leading to the town from a mountain lake. The Atlanteans had airships powered by the anti-gravity technology that could seat two to eight people. The economic system was socialist, like that of the Incas. The Atlanteans were the first to develop organized warfare. The military deployed vril-powered air battleships that contained 50 to 100 fighting men. These air battleships deployed poison gas bombs. The infantry fired fire-tipped arrows.

The Toltecs on Atlantis worshipped the Sun in temples as grand as those of ancient Egypt that were decorated in bright colors. The sacred word used in meditation was Tau (the equivalent of the Aryan sacred word AUM). As noted above, the

Toltecs colonized all of North America and South America and thus became the people we know as the Amerindians.

The downfall of Atlantis started when some of the Toltecs began to practice black magic around 850,000 BC, corrupted by the dragon "Thevetat," remembered as Devadatta, the opponent of Buddha. The people started to become selfish and materialistic. Soon after that, the Turonians (the ancestors of the people we now know as the Turkic peoples) became dominant in much of Atlantis. The Turonians continued the practice of black magic, which reached its height in about 250,000 BC and continued until the final sinking of Atlantis, although white magicians opposed them. Master Morya incarnated as the Emperor of Atlantis in 220,000 BC to counter the black magicians. The black magicians used magical spells to breed human-animal chimeras.

They possessed an army of chimeras composed of a human body with the heads of fierce predators, such as lions, tigers, and bears, which ate enemy corpses on the battlefield. The war between white and black magicians continued until the end of Atlantis. The Masters of the Ancient Wisdom telepathically warned their disciples (the white magicians) to flee Atlantis in ships while there was still time to get out before the final cataclysm. As noted above, the final sudden submergence of Atlantis due to earthquakes occurred in 9,564 BC.

Blavatsky asserted humanity is now in _the fifth or Aryan root race_, which Theosophists believe in having emerged from the previous fourth root race (Atlantean root race) beginning about 100,000 years ago in Atlantis. (According to Powell, when Madame Blavatsky stated the Aryan root race was 1,000,000 years old, she meant that the souls of the people that later physically incarnated as the first Aryans about 100,000 years ago began to incarnate in the bodies of Atlanteans 1,000,000 years ago. However, another way of interpreting this is that Nature started to create the Aryan race before the final cataclysms.) Theosophists believe the Vaivasvatu Manu physically progenerated the Aryan root race, one of the Masters of Ancient Wisdom, compared with Vaivasvata Manu of Hinduism.

Theosophists believe the Vaivasvatu Manu physically progenerated the Aryan root race, one of the Masters of Ancient Wisdom, compared with Vaivasvata Manu of Hinduism. The present-day ethnic group most closely related to the new race is the Kabyle. The small band of only 9,000 people constituting the small Aryan root race migrated out of Atlantis in 79,797 BC. The birds of the new white root-race poetically referred to the new race as *moon-colored*. A small group of these Aryan migrants from Atlantis split from the main body of migrants and went south to the shore of an inland

375

sea in what was then a verdant Sahara, where they founded the "City of the Sun."

The main body of migrants continued onwards to an island called the "white island" in the middle of what was then an inland sea in what is now the Gobi Desert, where they established the "City of the Bridge." (The "City of the Bridge" was constructed directly below the aetheric City called Shamballa, where Theosophists believe the governing deity of Earth, Sanat Kumara [compared with Sanat Kumaras of Hinduism], dwells; thus, the ongoing evolution of the Aryan root race has been divinely guided by the being Theosophists call "The Lord of the World.") The esoteric name of the whole of the present land surface of Earth, i.e., the World Island, the Americas, the Australian continent, and Antarctica, was taken is *Krauncha*. Blavatsky connects physical race with spiritual attributes constantly throughout her works:

376

The intellectual difference between the Aryan and other civilized nations and such savages as the South Sea Islanders is inexplicable on any other grounds. No amount of culture, nor generations of training amid civilization, could raise such human specimens as the Bushmen, the Veddhas of Ceylon, and some African tribes, to the same intellectual level as the Aryans, the Semites, and the Turonian's so-called - 'sacred spark' is missing in them, and they are the only inferior races on the globe, now happily – owing to the wise adjustment of Nature which, ever works in that direction – fast dying out. Humanity is 'of one blood,' but not of the same essence. We are the hot-house, artificially quickened plants in Nature, having in us a spark, which in them is latent.

Esoteric history teaches that idols and their worship died out with the Fourth Race until the survivors of the hybrid races of the latter (Chinamen, African Negroes, &c.) gradually

377

brought the worship back. The Vedas countenance no idols; all the modern Hindu writings do. Generally speaking, a large percentage of the people who live in the period of the fifth root race are part of the fifth root race.

However, Blavatsky also opines that some Semitic peoples have become "degenerate in spirituality." She asserted that some people descended from the Lemurians are "semi-animal creatures." These latter include "the Tasmanians, a portion of the Australians." There are also "considerable numbers of the mixed Lemuro-Atlantean peoples produced by various crossings with such semi-human stocks - e.g. the wild men of Borneo, the Veddhas of Ceylon, most of the remaining Australians, Bushmen, Negritos, Andaman Islanders, etc." All these groups mentioned above mentioned by Blavatsky, except the Borneans, are part of what, in the late 19th century and most of the 20th century, was called the

378

Australoid race (except for the Bushmen, part of the Capoid race), both of which races, as noted above, were believed by traditional Theosophists to have been descended from the Lemurians.

Blavatsky described the fifth root race with the following words: The Aryan races, for instance, now vary from dark brown, almost black, red-brown-yellow, down to the whitest creamy color, are yet all of the same stock — the Fifth Root Race — and spring from one single progenitor, who is said to have lived over 18,000,000 years ago, and also 850,000 years ago — at the time of the sinking of the last remnants of the great continent of Atlantis.

She also prophesies the destruction of the racial "failures of nature" as the future "higher race" ascends: Thus, will humanity, race after race, perform its appointed cycle pilgrimage? Climates will, and have already begun, to change, each tropical year after the other, dropping one sub-race, but only to beget another higher race on the ascending cycle, while a series of other less favored groups – the failures of Nature – will, like some individual men, vanish from the human family without even leaving a trace behind.

The subraces (which Steiner renamed "Cultural Epochs" as an adequate expression for our times) of the Aryan Fifth Root Race includes the first subrace the Hindu, which migrated from the "City of the Bridge" on the white island in the middle of the Gobi inland sea to India in 60,000 BC; the second subrace the Arabian, which migrated from the "City of the Bridge" to Arabia in 40,000 BC; the third subrace, the Persian, migrated from the "City of the Bridge" to Persia in 30,000 BC; the fourth subrace the Celts, which migrated from the "City of the Bridge" to Western Europe beginning in 20,000 BC (the Mycenaean Greeks are regarded as an offshoot of the Celtic sub-race that colonized Southeast Europe); and the fifth sub-race, the Teutonic, which also migrated from the "*City of the*

Bridge" to what is now Germany beginning in 20,000 BC (the Slavs are regarded as an offshoot of the Teutonic subrace that colonized Russia and surrounding areas).

The future *6th root race* will first come out of the United States of America. It will continue when the USA breaks up into smaller nations. Then, it will be the whole west coast, including Canada, Baja, Mexico, and Alaska, as the government will join with Australia and New Zealand with Pacific Islands; this will be the nation that will comprise the new sixth root race to lead the world. Many people in California will develop psychic skills soon. One day the pacific nation will rule the world under one government with the assistance of the great *Master Morya* and will incarnate physically to the Earth and lead. In the 28th century, they used *eugenics* to breed this new race overtime under the support of the great masters.

381

2. *Trends of governments.* The world has had many land empires in historical times. The Roman Empire led into the Germanic Empires with the Easter Roman Greek Empire, the French Napoleonic Empire, and the Spanish then American Empires. Now, the European Union and Canada can only get by with the USA supporting them. All these Empires were, and still are, established by the great masters and designed by them to create new cultures and peoples. One day, in the future, we will have a world government. The whole planet will be at peace, and there will be no poor or rich people. This world order will be based roughly on the communist manifesto but modernized in a capitalized market.

3. *Trend is thought, Art, Architecture, and fashion.* All these minor trends reflect world events. These little trends are human-related and subject to the human condition. There have been many developing trends in thought and government. The result is for the happiness of the people. Humanity

382

under the royals was very oppressed; Napolitano Buonaparte and his brother Louis Napoléon Bonaparte finally ended that. Louis Napoléon Bonaparte enlarged Paris to be a world city. He broadened many roads and created a new architecture for a new Paris. Louis brought France into the modern age. All of Europe followed the example set by Louis. Now we are in the modern era. Wars are still not thought of in the past, as we know from the Ukrainian/Russian war or 2021 to the present.

In the Art world, we went from the Proto-Renaissance to the 1300s with their gothic art and architecture, to the Renaissance, to baroque, to the romantic period, to impressionist, post-impressionist, expressionist, Avant Gard, to cubic art, to futuristic art, to abstract expressionist, to photorealistic art, to now. Art has taken many turns due to social reactions to world fairs. We can say

383

the same about philosophy and psychology, too, with many periods of discoveries and growth.

Performing this magic would open your Mind to many new ideas and ways to use the Mind in general. To do this magic or meditation: Lay out a white tablecloth with a black candle in its center. Draw a black teardrop egg on the candle's glass with a blue ball in the center. Chant *Akasha Akasha* four times, twice a day, until the candle burns out.

One last thought about the writing of Theosophy, those civilizations existed on various astral planes and not on this physical earth.

Akasha Akasha or the Aetheric Part of Aether

The Aetheric part of Aether is the highest study in this alchemical Hindu philosophy. We are talking about pure spirit here with no contaminations from the four lower elements; this will take us to the ninth Dimension, as a matter of fact. All lower Dimensions are of the five elements. For the rest of this chapter, I will reference my earlier work – *Personal growth in the multi-dimensional multiverse.*

In that book, I wrote about the thirty-three Dimensions and even higher as a means of personal growth. I wrote about the ridiculous riddles we seem to attract to solve in coming to understand God Himself. We always fail at trying to solve these riddles, but we seem to continue in vain anyway. We draw these ridiculous riddles of who God is, not for us to understand but to relax and accept who we are and who God truly is. We come to these riddles in the Chaos of our doubt that God hid something from us. We came to mistrust God and, thus, fell into Chaos. This Chaos holds ridiculous riddles about who God is as a way for us to make up for the doubts we have about Him or to be equal with Him so nothing can be hidden from us.

All these notions are out of fear and mistrust. We caused a rebellion in heaven and were thrown out of it. We are, in fact, the demons who are cast out of heaven. We created this story and projected the enemy onto fictional characters – called demons. To return home we are the demons that were cast out of heaven. We must- relax and know that we are at one with God now. The devil is our self-consciousness and our rebellion away from God. If this is so, our leader must be the devil as they all have self-consciousnesses. Now, who or what is the Devil? The devil makes himself known to us, utilizing our consciousness. We got our consciousness through this devil.

386

Even our current riddle of life is devilish – we can know God by being gods here. So, where is salvation? The Fact is, we can return to God's graces by being at one with all things and to know that we are at one with God. I also mentioned earlier that we can never reach God but to enjoy the journey back to Him. True, but to be truly at one with God is to be the drop of water in the ocean of life that becomes the ocean itself. This is the closest explanation I can write about being at one with God – all things. You can even do it right now!

Back to consciousness a bit, it won't be until the thirteen-Dimension, when we have finally dropped our consciousness, that we will fully understand God. In the fourteen Dimensions, we can construct ourselves as a new spirit of God. Our universe is highly attuned to the fourteen-Dimension as spirits of God feel for men of God, or men who want to be as God. Our universal Logi is of the fourteen Dimension. He intends to bring us to

387

his level and beyond if possible and to be that drop of water that becomes the ocean.

This ends my part on the Tattva now.

This last part of this book is dedicated to the four Gunasas:

- Sattva – sweet, good, holy, consciousness.

- A-Sattva – beyond good, discipline, the unconscious beyond awareness of the universe.

- Raja - leadership, anger, fighting, action.

- Tamas – stability, structures, negative, restrictive.

Why are the Four Gunas important to understand?

Gunas are qualities of nature. To understand them, we have to find our balance in life. The Gunas (Sanskrit for strands or qualities) are energetic forces that weave together to form the universe and everything in it. There are three Gunas, each with its unique attributes: tamas (stability), rajas (activity), and sattva (consciousness). It might help to think of Gunas as tendencies: the habitual ways you respond to any situation that arises.

All three Gunas are present in every experience in a constantly shifting relationship with one another. One quality is always more present or dominant than the others, depending on your challenge – and, most importantly, how you respond to it. When you overreact because someone cuts you off in traffic, rajas become dominant. If you emotionally shut down to avoid having a difficult conversation, that's a sign that tamas has taken the reins. As you emerge from a beautiful restorative practice, you may experience the sattvic quality of joy. Understanding the Gunas is essential because while the challenges of our everyday lives can disturb their delicate balance, these energies, entwined in an intricate dance, create all that we are, all that we see, and all that remains unseen. Tamas provides our foundation; rajas give it vitality and breath; sattva imbues it with consciousness and compassionate awareness.

In the philosophy of Yoga, all matter in the universe arises from the fundamental substrate called Prakriti. From this ethereal Prakriti the three primary Gunas (qualities of energy) emerge creating the essential aspects of all nature—energy, matter, and consciousness. These three Gunas are tamas (darkness & chaos), rajas (activity & passion), and sattva (beingness & harmony). The awareness and conscious manipulation of the three

390

Gunas are a powerful way to reduce stress, increase
inner peace and lead one towards enlightenment.

What is a Gunas?

Guna is a Sanskrit word which translates as "quality, peculiarity, attribute, or tendency." In yoga and Ayurveda, a Guna is a Tattva or element of reality that can affect our psychological, emotional, and energetic states. The three Gunas were created as an essential component of Sankhya philosophy but the gunas are now a major concept in most schools of Indian philosophy. The three Gunas are described as being constantly influx and interacting with one another, in a playful state referred to as maya or illusion. The patterns of the interplay of the Gunas can define the essential qualities of someone or something, and these patterns can highly influence the path and progress of life. For yoga practitioners, awareness of the Gunas provides a GPS to allow us to make choices to be more balanced, peaceful and harmonious both on and off our mat. Cultivating the ability to identify and understand the nature of the Gunas brings us closer to seeing the universal truth of oneness.

The three Gunas:
Tamas, Rajas, and Sattva

All three Gunas are always present in all beings and objects surrounding us but vary in their relative amounts. We humans have the unique ability to consciously alter the levels of the Gunas in our bodies and minds. The Gunas cannot be separated or removed in oneself but can be consciously acted upon to encourage their increase or decrease. A Guna can be increased or decreased through the interaction and influence of external objects, lifestyle practices and thoughts.

Qualities of the three Gunas

Tamas is a state of darkness, inertia, inactivity, and materiality. Tamas manifests from ignorance and deludes all beings from their spiritual truths. Other tamasic qualities are laziness, disgust,

393

attachment, depression, helplessness, doubt, guilt, shame, boredom, addiction, hurt, sadness, apathy, confusion, grief, dependency, ignorance.

Rajas is a state of energy, action, change, and movement. The nature of rajas is of attraction, longing and attachment and rajas strongly bind us to the fruits of our work. Other rajasic qualities are anger, euphoria, anxiety, fear, irritation, worry, restlessness, stress, courage, rumination, determination, chaos.

Sattva is a state of harmony, balance, joy, and intelligence. Sattva is the guna that yogis achieve towards as it reduces rajas and tamas and thus makes liberation possible. Other sattvic qualities are delight, happiness, peace, wellness, freedom, love, compassion, equanimity, empathy, friendliness, focus, self-control, satisfaction, trust, fulfillment, calmness, bliss, cheerfulness, gratitude, fearlessness, selflessness.

Rajas	Sattva	Tamas
Activity	*Truth / Goodness*	*Inertia & inactivity*
Passion, desire & attachment	Light, harmony & balance	Darkness, delusion & ignorance
Energy	Spiritual Essence	Mass / matter / heaviness
Expansion	Upward flow	Downward flow
Movement	Intelligence & consciousness	Sloth & dullness
Binds by means of passion and craving.	Binds by means of attachment to knowledge and joy.	Binds by means of ignorance and obstruction.

Working With the Gunas

The mind's psychological qualities are highly unstable and can quickly fluctuate between the different Gunas. The predominant Guna of the mind acts as a lens that affects our perceptions and perspective of the world around us. Thus, if the Mind is in rajas, it will experience world events as chaotic, confusing, and demanding and it will then have a strong tendency to continue to react to events in a rajasic way. Therefore, for yogis to make progress along the path we must practice self-observation and discernment to witness and not react to the activities of the Gunas. We must also have the inner-strength and willpower to consciously shift our thoughts and actions away from tamas and rajas towards sattvic balance and purpose.

To reduce tamas, avoid tamasic foods, oversleeping, overeating, inactivity, passivity, and fearful situations. Tamasic foods include heavy meats and foods that are spoiled, chemically treated, processed, or refined.

To reduce rajas, avoid rajasic foods, over-exercising, overwork, loud music, excessive thinking, and consuming excessive material goods. Rajasic foods include fried foods, spicy foods, and stimulants. For more info read Reducing Rajas Guna: A Yogi's How-To Guide.

To increase sattva, reduce both rajas and tamas, eat sattvic foods and enjoy activities and environments that produce joy and positive thoughts. Sattvic foods include whole grains and legumes and fresh fruits and vegetables that grow above the ground. All the yogic practices were developed to create sattva in the mind and body. Thus, practicing yoga and leading a yogic lifestyle strongly cultivates sattva.

All Gunas create attachment and thus bind oneself to the ego. "When one rises above the three Gunas originating in the body; one is freed from

397

birth, old age, disease, and death; and attains enlightenment" (Bhagavad Gita 14.20). While the yogi's goal is to cultivate sattva, his or her goal is to transcend their misidentification of the self with the Gunas and to be unattached to both the good and the bad, the positive and negative qualities of all life.

What is A-Sattva? A-Sattva is balance, harmony, goodness, purity, universalizing, holistic, constructive, creative, building, positive attitude, luminous, serenity, being-ness, peaceful, virtuous, goodness beyond our understandings. It is associated with karma, either good or bad. A-Sattva is discipline, and oppressions coming if you are out of harmony with nature. A–Sattva is there to remind us to face our misdeeds head on and to learn from them. A-Sattva can explain why bad things happen to a person, group, race, nation, or a world. If we are small minded, we will not understand why these chaotic things are happening. Only a very deeply intuitive mind could be able to find out why these things are happening. The holocaust happened for a certain reason – it was karmic. The souls that died during the holocaust killed others in a way that they were killed. We need A -Sattva so we can work hard to go great thinks in this world. We need it to build character in virtues that we did not have before.

At first there were just two gunas – Sattva and Tamas. Raja was not present until the spirit was introduced to the two. Lastly, A-Sattva came along to make the three productive, holy, pure, and constructive. Yes, in the beginning it was like black and white like the Tattva of Akasha – Black & White. Agni is akin to Raja which created the four gunas form the pure fire of Agni/Raja. You can even say that tamas is akin to Prithvi and Sattva to Apas while we have A-Sattva to Akasha. These are akin however the gunas came eons before the universe was created.

Paramathma and the Scriptures drastically depart from conventional thought regarding how the

Universe was created. Remember, the perceived Universe is only a reflection of the qualities of the inner self. It is to be read as a reflection to enable the Atma to evolve and shed dependence on the physical self.

So, since the Universe is only an instrument of the forces of consciousness, including the Mind, the Universe is said to be formed due to the imbalances of the forces in the Jiva Atma and its main instrument, the Mind.

To apply a bit of modern physics, forces come into existence only due to imbalances. If there was a perfect balance, no forces would be created or come into play. The power behind Perception is the ATMA. ATMA, when completely balanced, is in Moksham State. But when or more of the three Gunas (Rajasic, Sattvic, Tamasic) begins to dominate, the ATMA becomes attached to the physical world through the sense organs and, more importantly, through the Mind.

What causes Perception to be born in a state of imbalance? What is the imbalance that renders the ATMA to perceive this Universe?

Concluding Thoughts

A quote from Rumi, a (Persian Poet 1207 – 1273) – "Lose Yourself".

"Lose Yourself"

Lose yourself, lose yourself in this love.

When you lose yourself in this love,

you will find everything.

Lose yourself, lose yourself.

Do not fear this loss,

For you will rise from the earth

and embrace the endless heavens.

Lose yourself, lose yourself.

Escape from this earthly form,

for this body is a chain

and you are its prisoner.

Smash through the prison wall

and walk outside with the kings and princes.

Lose yourself,

Lose yourself at the foot of the glorious King.

When you lose yourself

before the King you will become the King.

Lose yourself, lose yourself.
Escape from the black cloud that surrounds you.
Then you will see your own light
as radiant as the full moon.

Now enter that silence. This is the surest way to
lose yourself. What is your life about, anyway?
Nothing but a struggle to be someone,
Nothing but a running from your own silence.

The most profound part of this poem is: *Nothing but struggle to be someone;* nothing, but the ruining of your own inner peace. The struggle of be someone in this world will take you from your true inner peace. In other words – just be you! The very simple you of who you are!

The next and last famous quote from Rumi is – "In Silence".

In Silence

A guide has entered this life in silence. His
message is only heard in silence.

Take a sip of his precious wine and lose yourself.
Don't insult the greatness of his love,
For he helps all those who suffer, in silence.

Polish the mirror between the breaths. Go with
him, beyond words. He knows your every deed. He
is the one who moves the wheel of heaven, in
silence.

Every thought is buried in your heart; He will
reveal them one by one, in silence.

Turn each of your thoughts into a bird And let
them fly to the other world. One is an owl, one is a
falcon, one is a crow. Each one is different from
the others, but they are all the same in silence.

To see the Moon that cannot be seen you must turn
your eyes inward and look at yourself, in silence.
In this world and the next, don't talk about this

and that; Let him show you everything, shining as one... in silence.

St. Thérèse de Lisieux - quotes are below!

"Holiness consists simply in doing God's will and being just what God wants us to be."

— St. Thérèse de Lisieux.

"The splendor of the rose and the whiteness of the lily do not rob the little violet of its scent or the daisy of its simple charm. If every tiny flower wanted to be a rose, spring would lose its loveliness."

— St. Therese of Lisieux

"Miss no single opportunity of making some small sacrifice, here by a smiling look, there by a kindly word; always doing the smallest right and doing it all for love."

— St. Therese of Lisieux

"Let me not have my rewards in heaven but let me have my heaven on earth serving others in need."

— St. Therese of Lisieux

"For me, prayer is a surge of the heart; it is a simple look turned toward heaven, it is a cry of recognition and of love, embracing both trial and joy."

— St. Therese of Lisieux

From St Therese of Lisieux, we learn that it is fine just to be the simple you, as Rumi mentioned, but to take every opportunity to do what is right and loving and to pray for the love you have for others. God's will be for us to be who we are now simply! God accepts us for who we are now. God's love for us is perfect; we should never doubt God. Such doubt brought us to these chaotic realms where we try to make sense of it all in our acts.

"Be still and know that we are at one with God."

- Edgar Cayce.

"Dreams are today's answers to tomorrow's questions."

- Edgar Cayce

"You can never lose anything that really belongs to you, and you can't keep that which belongs to someone else."

-Edgar Cayce

"It is thought and feeling which guides the universe, not deeds."

-Edgar Cayce

"There is progress whether ye are going forward or backward! The thing is to move!"

-Edgar Cayce

"For, he that expects nothing shall not be disappointed, but he that expects much - if he lives and uses that in hand day by day - shall be full to running over."

-Edgar Cayce

"When ye are prepared for a thing, the opportunity to use it presents itself."

407

-Edgar Cayce

From what Edgar Cayce is saying, reality in life is aetheric and not what we think it is. We are always forwarded of life in our dreams and even if we seem to make a mistake, it is all a process anyway and an important one just to get there. Try not to expect too much from life or life will prove to be hard. Anything that is right for you will happen on its own.

St. Teresa of Avila, pray for us! – read them below.

"Accustom yourself continually to make many acts of love, for they enkindle and melt the soul."

"You pay God a compliment by asking great things of Him."

"There are more tears shed over answered prayers than over unanswered prayers."

"Christ has no body now but mine. He prays in me, works in me, looks through my eyes, speaks through

my words, works through my hands, walks with my feet, and loves with me here."

"From silly devotions and sour-faced saints, good Lord, deliver us!"

"The surest way to determine whether one possesses the love of God is to see whether he or she loves his or her neighbor. These two loves are never separated. Rest assured, the more you progress in love of neighbor, the more your love of God will increase."

"You must trust God that you are exactly where you are meant to be now."

"God walks among the pots and the pans."

"We always find that those who walked closest to Christ were those who had to bear the greatest trials."

"We shall never learn to know ourselves except by endeavoring to know God; for, beholding his greatness, we realize our own littleness; his purity

409

shows us our foulness; and by meditating upon his humility, we find how very far we are from being humble."

From what St Teresa of Avilla is saying, you honor God with your prayer. To be of God is to treat others the way you do yourselves. All your matters should be brought to prayer.

My closing comment on this Chapter is from Edgar Cayce:

"Just be still and know that you are at one with God."

Author's Biography

My Author's biography – Regarding my writer's personal education in qualifying me to write my two books, I was always very intuitive even in my youth and was a religious young boy who knew the Bible. After the army, I got involved in spiritualism and the occult with Tarot, Runes, Numerology, and Astrology.

I find Egyptian mythology and its magical religion fascinating and am a student of all New Aged brands of study. Later, I took my spiritual study more seriously and became both a Theosophist and Christian Scientist – not Scientology as I must say, many confuse the two. The best divination skill I possessed was always automatic writing. In fact, I wrote my two books using that very skill. My metaphysical background was helpful but not always relied upon.

Many people called me a walking encyclopedia of metaphysics. In this manner, I feel

411

that I am very qualified to write my alternative spirituality books. My recent interest in quantum physicals and higher math formed the framework for my current book on the multiverse, and my older spiritual experiences for the Enigma of God. When I write intuitively, I have no idea what I am writing or know of its source, but I simply feel it is truthful. I ask you now to trust my abilities and foreknowledge and read my two Balboa press books.

Born in metropolitan New Jersey/ New York area in August of 1961, I grew up in New Jersey with beautiful memories that I still look back on. I was a religious boy and kept out of trouble for the most part. I left traditional religions due to sexual reasons and more freedom. After college, at age 25, I joined the Army, then I became a disabled Veteran and had to be discharged; I was a rebellious soldier and had to be discharged; I was very rebellious and chaotic, further in New York City in my 20s to 40s.

After my military service, I moved to New York City in 1988. Before the army I would only take trips from New Jersey to the big city – NYC. I worked for Virgin Atlantic airlines in reservations for four years and traveled extensively after my army days. I was understood by that airline to be the most extensive traveler from 1990 to 1993.

Studied all formed by the New Age movement studies and completed my knowledge with Theosophy and Christian Science in New York City in the 90's to the millennium. I am currently an Astrologer, tarot, and rune reader. I have worked many psychic phone lines in my time and still do.

My best skill is automatic writing. I wrote two books using that skill of writing. All the information in those two books was intuitively written and original to me. I do not study metaphysics anymore, apart from astrology updates all my mystical knowledge comes from my intuitive automotive writings by means of my inner light.

413

Apart from that, quantum theory and higher math interest me. My goal is to understand quantum mechanics in a mathematical written form one day – the multiverse was my first attempt at doing so.

Astrophysics does interest me a lot. Did you know that the force with which our Suns pull on our planet is three times the weight of all our oceans? We are only drawn to the Sun by 1/3 of a millimeter per year due to this draw! Our rotation around our Sun is that strong! Did you know?

My two books

My first book was "The Enigma of God, revelation to man – Balboa press in 2009. Then, I wrote "Personal growth in the multi-dimensional multiverse in 2021 with Balboa Press again. My author's biography in my first book – The enigma of God, was a bit dated; now it is complete on this website.

My second book "Personal Growth in the multi-dimensional multiverse" 2022 Balboa press is about quantum physics as it pertains to personal growth.

Other interests

I recorded 15 songs in English and Italian, mostly in Miami and a few in New Orleans with many of my composed instrumental ballets on fl Studio and a few musical notation programs in New Orleans to the present. I am currently working on two sheet music books, one for the harp and the other for the violin. I enjoy singing in the church choir and volunteer choirs as well.

It is my pleasure to play the piano, violin, and harp, though I am best at the violin; however, composing many new and original songs on piano and harp to sing to is my pastime. New Orleans is a city of music, and I go out to enjoy jazz often with some burlesque too. I then moved to Miami Beach in 2013 from New York City, and finally, moved to New Orleans in 2018. New York City after the Army was a big eye-opener for me! My worldly experiences in New York City are beyond any of my words' explanations.

Glad to be fully vaccinated and never had HIV, regardless of a decadent past in New York City in my 20s to 40s; I live in peace with a Persian cat named Baby. I plan to have my first child soon; now, do support a new author by buying two today if you may!!!